Cooperative Development

Professional self-development
through
cooperation with colleagues

Julian Edge

Longman Group UK Limited,
Longman House, Burnt Mill, Harlow,
Essex CM20 2JE, England
and Associated Companies throughout the world.

Distributed in the United States of America by Longman Publishing, New York.

© Longman Group UK Limited 1992

First published 1992
ISBN 0 582 06465 1

British Library Cataloguing in Publication Data

Edge, Julian
  Cooperative Development: Professional
  Self-development Through Cooperation
  with Colleagues
  I. Title
  650.1

  ISBN 0-582-06465-1

Library of Congress Cataloging-in-Publication Data

Edge, Julian, 1948–
  Cooperative development: professional self-development through
  cooperation with colleagues/Julian Edge.
    p. cm. – (Teacher to teacher)
  Includes bibliographical references (p. 104).
  ISBN 0-582-06465-1
  1. English language–Study and teaching–Foreign speakers.
  2. English teachers–Training of. I. Title. II. Series.
  PE1128.A2E27 1992
  428'.007–dc20   91-45772
                                         CIP

Set in 10/12pt Cheltenham ITC Light
Printed in Hong Kong
WC/01

Acknowledgements

We are grateful to the following for permission to reproduce copyright material;

The British Council for the article 'The least we can do is write to each other' by Julian Edge from *Focus on English*, Vol 6, No 1 (January 1990); Butterworth-Heinemann Ltd for a simplified inventory from *Management Teams: Why They Succeed or Fail* by Belbin (1981), © Belbin, 1981; Paul Chapman Publishing Ltd for page 56 and an adapted and simplified extract from *Effective School Management* by K B Everard and G Morris (second edition, 1990); HarperCollins Publishers for a slightly adapted questionnaire from *Managing Change and Making It Stick* by R Plant (Fontana, 1987); International Association of Teachers of English as a Foreign Language for the articles 'Research and Development' by Julian Edge from *IATEFL Teacher Development Special Interest Group Newsletter*, Issue 7, 1987 and 'No proof, no disproof: the search for authenticity' by Julian Edge from *IATEFL Teacher Development Special Interest Group Newsletter*, Issue 8, 1988; Bob Marley/Blue Mountain Music for an extract from the lyrics of the song 'Redemption Song' by Bob Marley.

We are grateful to the following for their permission to reproduce copyright illustrations:

Body Language by Allan Pease, © Allan Pease, Sheldon Press & Bantom Doubleday/Dell Publishing Group, Inc. for pages 25 and 94. © 1983 by Marilee Zdenek. Extracted from 'The Right Brain Experience', by Corgi Books. All rights reserved, for page 57.

CONTENTS

None but ourselves can free our minds.
Bob Marley

PART 1
Introduction

This is a book for teachers. Because teaching can take up a lot of our lives in one way or another, an increasing number of us want to find out more about ourselves, our teaching and the relationship between the two. Then we ask ourselves, how can we use what we discover to guide our future development? In individual terms, how can I become the best teacher I can be for my students?

This goal of working out our own way forward, based on our own understanding, is often referred to as *empowerment*. Cooperative Development is the framework for empowerment that I want to offer.

Workshops with numerous groups of teachers in Brazil, India, Japan, Pakistan and Poland, as well as with multinational groups in Britain, suggest that Cooperative Development can function in a wide variety of cultural contexts.

The short term outcome for participants is usually an increase in their:

- awareness of their own strengths and skills;
- appreciation of the strengths and skills of others;
- willingness to listen carefully to others;
- ability to respond to the needs of their own teaching situation;
- confidence in their capacity to empower themselves.

The intended long term outcome is the implementation of a practical framework for continuing professional self-development.

This book is an attempt to reach yet more teachers. Part 1 presents the ideas which underpin Cooperative Development. Parts 2–4 involve you in a programme of activities aimed at personal awareness raising and the learning of the distinctive set of communicative skills which power Cooperative Development. Part 5 reviews further contexts of use for Cooperative Development and acknowledges the sources I have drawn on in putting this framework together.

I would like to add a word to those who have administrative control over teachers. Organisational development through the involvement and empowerment of the workforce is a constant feature of successful management. Institutions which support teachers in their cooperation and self-development will move into leading positions, both in terms of the quality of teaching they provide, and in the efficiency of its provision.

Good luck to us all.

1 What is Cooperative Development?

Individuals and colleagues

At the heart of teacher development is the idea of self-development.
This works at two levels.

Firstly, as an individual, my development is in my own hands. With
or without official training and education as a teacher, only I can
really understand what I am trying to do in class, how it works out
for me, and what I learn from it. If I follow this up, I can find a sense
of personal satisfaction in my work that goes beyond that great
feeling of 'having a really good lesson'. Every lesson can be a part of
finding out more about teaching, about learning and about myself.

Secondly, as members of different schools, or societies, or cultures,
only we have the insights of insiders into what is happening with our
learners in our classrooms. If we follow this up, it can take us away
from the frustration of seeing our teaching future defined by the
latest method, the latest guru, or the latest coursebook.

At both levels, of course, we can go on learning from others: from
in-service training courses, from visiting speakers, and from new (and
old) publications. But the idea that we should go on taking ideas
from others and applying them to our own situations meets only a
part of our potential. To serve our own *development*, we need a way
of working that encourages us to look more closely at ourselves and
to work on what we find.

At the same time this emphasis on self doesn't mean that we
should work in isolation. The isolation of the teacher is exactly what
holds us back. We all too regularly limit teaching to an individual,
subjective experience shared with no one. As a direct result of this,
we restrict our ability to develop as teachers, and we hand over to
outsiders important questions about what good teaching is and how
it might be assessed.

I want to investigate and assess my own teaching. I can't do that
without understanding it better, and I can't understand it on my own.
Here, we are close to the heart of a paradox. When I use the word
development, I always mean *self-development*. But that can't be done
in isolation. Self-development needs other people: colleagues and

3

students. By cooperating with others, we can come to understand better our own experiences and opinions. We can also enrich them with the understandings and experiences of others. Through cooperation, we have a chance to escape from simple, egocentric subjectivity, without chasing after a non-existent objectivity.

I need someone to work with, but I don't need someone who wants to change me and make me more like the way they think I ought to be. I need someone who will help me see myself clearly. To make this possible, we need a distinct style of working together so that each person's development remains in that person's own hands. This type of interaction will involve learning some new rules for speaking, for listening and for responding in order to cooperate in a disciplined way.

This mixture of awareness-raising and disciplined cooperation is what I have called *Cooperative Development*. Cooperative Development is a way of working together with someone in order to become a better teacher in your own terms.

Where can I use Cooperative Development?

As a way of working with someone, Cooperative Development has the potential to suit many teaching contexts and purposes. It can play a role in *pre-service training* and *in-service training*; it is particularly suited to collaborative *classroom research*, and it, or something like it, will become more and more important as teachers take increasing responsibility for the *assessment* of their own work. I have more to say about these different contexts in Chapter 14. In the meantime, I want to concentrate on the style of working interaction itself, as it can be used between two people committed to the idea of continuing professional development in their normal lives.

Here, then, there is no teacher training or teacher education element involved, in the sense that these imply a difference of status between people working together. This is a way of cooperation between equals. Two teachers cooperate in order to work on one person's (self-)development. That's what this is all about.

I hope it is becoming clear that this is a book for doing, as well as for reading. You can't understand what I'm trying to say by just reading the book. As you read, I hope that you'll want to try out the activities with a friend. Work with the ideas and see if they can work for you. After a while, you may find that you develop a cooperative style of your own. If you find a way to cooperate and develop which suits you, whatever the details of that cooperation are, this book will have achieved its purpose.

Towards activity

If you are going to get the most out of this book, you will be thinking about getting involved in some active cooperation with at least one colleague. I once heard someone say, 'Teachers don't have colleagues, just other people who work at the same place'. At the time, I thought that it was a clever thing to have said. As time has passed, the importance of that distinction has become central to my thinking on teaching and on my own development as a teacher. Here is one set of associations with the word 'colleague':

aider, ally, assistant, associate, auxiliary, collaborator, companion, comrade, confederate, confrère, fellow worker, helper, partner, team mate, workmate.

The New Collins Thesaurus (1984:107)

There is a richness here from which we could all benefit. Think about the people you work with. Who do you trust, or could you come to trust, enough to want to share your thoughts and ideas with them? Who would you be prepared to invite into your class now and again to watch you teach? Not so that they could evaluate your teaching, but so that they would know exactly what you mean when you talk about your teaching.

Please make sure that you at least talk to one or two people about these ideas. It's time to get ready.

2 Learning and knowing

In the last chapter, I talked about how we can learn from books and experts, and how we can learn from our own experience. These are two different ways of learning and I believe that they produce different types of knowledge.

The former type of learning is a mainly cognitive process which produces *intellectual comprehension*. I have this kind of knowledge of how a light bulb works, of why millions must starve every year on our rich planet, of what the teacher does in a Suggestopedia class.

The latter type of learning involves at least as much of an emotional process which produces *experiential understanding*. I have this kind of knowledge of how it feels to be called 'Daddy', of what it is like to be threatened at gunpoint, of why Community Language Learning classes can be difficult to get going.

I don't want to get tied up in the pastime of giving new technical meanings to everyday words, so I'm not going to continue to use *comprehension* and *understanding* in this differential way. But I hope that this distinction between intellectual learning and experiential learning, between intellectual knowing and experiential knowing is an acceptable one.

If you think about in-service teacher training, you might agree that one of the major problems is incompatibility between intellectual learning and experiential knowledge. That is to say, it sometimes seems to be the case that what we are told by a trainer, or learn from a book, just does not gel with what we know to be true from our own experience. It is very difficult to bring the two forms of learning and knowledge together.

To make progress on this front, we need to turn to a third dimension of learning and knowing; a dimension which is not sufficiently recognised in education systems. It is easy to accept the idea that we learn from experience and by taking in ideas from other people. It is now time to remind ourselves of an opposite and equally true principle:

We learn by speaking: by trying to put our thoughts together so that someone else can understand them.

A lot of what we think we know is a jumble of unexamined information and feelings. When I try to put my thoughts into a coherent shape, as I have to if I am going to communicate them to someone else, I often find that my ideas are less clear than I thought they were. And I find that my opinions are not always as solidly founded as I wish they were. I find, then, that my ideas need developing, my plans need sharpening up.

There is another, more positive angle on this experience. Sometimes, it is exactly when I am trying to formulate my ideas that I see properly for the first time just exactly how they do fit together: by exploring my thoughts, I discover something new. That 'something new' may well be the basis for a new plan of action that will move me along in an interesting direction.

Finally, it is in my attempts to express myself – to express my *self* – that I bring together my intellectual knowledge and my experiential knowledge in a way that obliges me to fuse the two into one person's integrated statement: mine. Experience and book-learning can drift along their separate ways indefinitely, but a serious attempt to articulate an individual opinion or position will bring the two together. And when I have made the statement that brings together my intellectual comprehension and my experiential understanding, I shall also have a much clearer idea of what I need to do next, whether that means gathering more experience, or reading another book.

There is an old joke in which someone says, 'How do I know what I think until I hear what I say?' What I mean by Cooperative Development obliges us to take that joke seriously.

You can probably see from the stress I have put on the importance of expressing oneself to someone else, that the role of the cooperating colleague comes in here. So, let's think of one teacher as the Speaker, and a colleague as the Understander. By making every effort to understand the Speaker, the Understander assists the Speaker's development. The role of the colleague in Cooperative Development is to help the Speaker develop the Speaker's own ideas by clarifying them and following them where they lead.

Let's be quite clear about this: I have nothing against a healthy exchange of opinions, nothing against passing on a bit of advice and nothing against someone showing me how to do something. All these have a role to play in being a teacher and being a colleague. But these are not the processes that we are involved in here. I am suggesting a deliberately different way of behaving, of speaking and of listening. This way of behaving requires a lot of discipline, because it is different from our usual ways of interacting. Cooperative Development is carried out in the roles of Speaker and Understander for an agreed period of time, or until participants agree to stop.

It won't be what we think of as 'natural' interaction, but that's because 'natural' is a misleading word.

In the next chapter, we shall spend a little time thinking about usual forms of interaction, and then go on to suggest some changes towards the purposes we have in mind.

What we have established in this chapter is the importance of three ways of learning:

- through our experience;
- through our intellect;
- through the formulation and expression of our ideas.

Cooperative Development focuses on the power of learning through expression.

Towards activity

Take a little time to think back and supply your own examples of what you have learned intellectually and what you have learned through experience.

As you think of your own examples, you will also note that it's not always easy to keep the two categories separate. They are different, but they affect each other.

In each case, try to formulate for yourself exactly what you learned and what you know and think about that topic now. How do you feel about those learning experiences?

3 Ways of interacting

When two people sit and talk together, certain norms are followed. This isn't usually a conscious matter. Nor is it natural. The norms are social, learned as a part of growing up in a speech community. In conversations and discussions in my culture, for example, the concentration is usually on what one is going to say oneself, and on how one is going to fit it in to the interaction. There is plenty of room for individual variation inside these norms, and such variation is part of the basis for some people being referred to as dour, hesitant, talkative, pushy, bossy, or downright rude.

If we think of a conversation in terms of space for ideas and talk, two people will usually share the space between them on a roughly equal basis. How equal will depend on such individual differences as we have mentioned above, on differences in knowledge, and on a shared idea of what is polite. Roughly speaking, we might think of a conversation like this:

Conversation

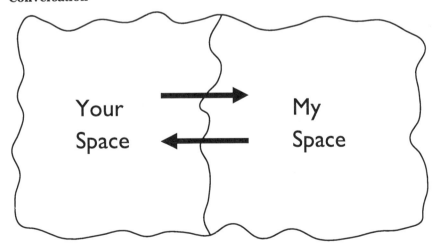

In a competitive interaction, such as a discussion, the stronger ideas, or those put forward most successfully, will tend to take up most space, as shown overleaf:

Discussion

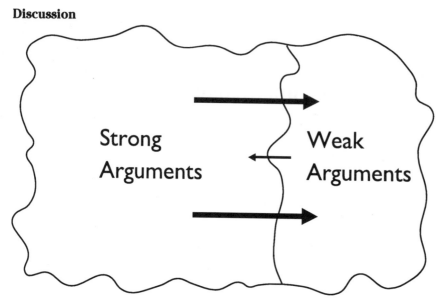

When we talk to people from other social groups, norms of interaction may differ. This is even more likely to occur when we converse across cultural boundaries, even if we appear to share a common language.

Whatever rules you are used to, I am asking you to suspend them. What I want to introduce is a new set of norms for face-to-face interaction. Not a complete set of rules, of course, but enough to shape a way of interacting with a colleague that seems particularly useful when the aim is to encourage independent self-development.

In Cooperative Development, the Understander deliberately sets out to make as much space as possible for the Speaker while, at the same time, actively working to help the Speaker use that space creatively.

Cooperative Development

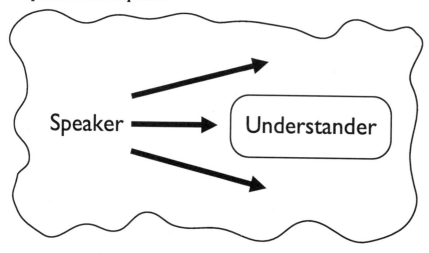

Cooperative Development depends totally on the idea of an agreement between two people to work together for a certain period of time according to rules that they both understand and agree on. As their work together continues, they may want to renegotiate the rules, but common understanding and agreement remain essential.

We shall soon look at the details of this interaction, but we need to begin with some underlying attitudes on which Cooperative Development has to be based. The three principles that I list below are qualities that the interaction between Speaker and Understander must have for Cooperative Development to take place. These, too, have to be talked about by the colleagues concerned until they share an agreement of how these principles function for them.

Respect

Firstly, the Understander accepts the Speaker's decision on what should be talked about and worked on. You may see a class of mine and think that I really need to work on the way I use pairwork. But if I want to work on how I correct pronunciation, you accept that decision out of respect for my feelings about where I can best develop right now.

Secondly, the Understander accepts what the Speaker has to say and accepts the Speaker's evaluations, opinions and intentions without judging them according to the Understander's knowledge or values. As Speaker, you may want to talk about a better way than you now have of allowing class time for student correction of written work. I may have already tried letting students correct written work in class and may be quite convinced that it is a complete waste of time. But as Understander, I must put my experiences aside and accept the validity of your hopes and aims.

We are working for the development of the Speaker's ideas. The Speaker needs to feel that these ideas can be pursued safely as they start to flow, without their being attacked if they show some weakness to someone else, or because someone else has other views.

One essential attitude for the Understander to have, then, is non-judgmental respect for the Speaker's views. Colleagues have every right to their views on teaching and students; they come out of their own experience and understanding. Development can only take place when Speakers recognise their own real views, and then see something in there which they wish to investigate, or to take further, or to change. Mutual, non-evaluative respect is fundamental to Cooperative Development.

Empathy

It is not enough for the Understander to respect the Speaker's right
to hold different views on teaching, or to teach classes in different
ways than the Understander would. In order to assist the Speaker's
development, the Understander has to try to see things through the
Speaker's eyes, to understand the classroom, the learning and the
teaching in the Speaker's frames of reference. Through an act of
acceptance and imagination, the Understander enters the world of the
Speaker. When I understand you, I make every effort to get into your
shoes, share your experiences, experience your feelings, and adopt
your objectives.

As the Understander attempts to empathise with the Speaker, the
Understander will have to ask for more and more clarification, and
the Speaker will work to make everything as clear as possible.
Equally important is catching the attitudinal and emotional tone of
what is being said. For example, it is important that you understand
that I don't use quiz games in my classes. But if you understand
from what I tell you that I loathe and detest quiz games, we might
have something more interesting to talk about.

Is it true that I feel this way? Is 'loathe' the best word to describe
my feelings? Why is that so? What exactly do other people think they
get from quiz games? Do I get that from something else in my
teaching? Are my students missing out? Is it time I tried such a quiz
(again)? As Speaker, it is when I can see and hear my own position
clearly in a supportive environment that I am best placed to evaluate
whether or not I like what I see, and best placed to judge where I
want to go next.

The quality of empathy, then, is one which the Understander tries
to develop in cooperation with the Speaker. It is something we aim
to get better at, rather than something we expect to achieve totally.
It is also something easier to experience than to understand or
explain.

Honesty

According to the previous two sections, the Understander aims to
accept what the Speaker says without evaluating or judging it in the
Understander's terms. Further, the Understander aims to empathise
with the Speaker and to enter the Speaker's world.

So, if I am telling you about how and why I make students
memorise lists of words each night, and you don't think that that is
a useful activity at all, it is your task to accept my evaluation of
word-lists, and see their use from my perspective.

Where does honesty come into this? Are you not being dishonest
by not pointing out to me what you *really* think about word-lists?

No. We are consciously operating here according to a different set
of rules, understood by both of us. For as long as we agree to work

together in this way, your role is to respect my ideas and try to empathise with my position.

What would be dishonest, would be if you only appeared to be respecting my ideas and empathising with me in order to manipulate me. Honesty is when you are genuine about your respect and empathy. Dishonesty is when you are stringing me along in order to bring me round to your way of thinking in the end. I can only develop from where I am; it is your role to help me see where I am in my own light. If using word-lists is such a bad idea, it will become apparent to me when I work on it. If it does not become apparent to me, you have to accept that it is not a bad idea for me.

I have tried above to lay out the necessary conditions of respect, empathy and honesty. In Part 2, I describe the style of interaction in terms of the actual techniques or abilities that one needs to develop. I shall describe nine such abilities, grouped into three blocks of three. They are introduced in this sequence as it suits their presentation and explanation. There is no suggestion that this represents a rigid order to be followed in a cooperative interaction. They are:

- **Exploration**
  Attending
  Reflecting
  Focusing

- **Discovery**
  Thematising
  Challenging
  Disclosing

- **Action**
  Goal-setting
  Trialling
  Planning.

Although much of this description relates necessarily to talk, we should remember that the purpose of development is action. The purpose of the talk is to help the Speaker decide on just what action would aid the Speaker's own potential development.

This book now also has to start doing a little more to live up to its promise of being a book for doing as well as for reading. All the chapters in Part 2 contain activities which are an essential part of what the book has to say. The final chapter of Part 1 presents some general comments which apply to all those activities.

Towards activity

Everyone knows that ideas can be worked out through discussion. Bad ideas can be identified and improved or jettisoned; good ideas can be made even better. I am not disputing this. I am suggesting that there is also another way forward, not replacing discussion, but adding to our possibilities.

To recap: for an agreed period, we deliberately abandon the element of argument and exchange that makes a discussion so useful. What we gain is a new experience of space into which one person's ideas can expand in the search for a discovery which might otherwise not have been made in the cut and thrust of argument.

When you're in a conversation, try to notice at what stage of listening to someone else you decide what it is you're going to say next. How long do you then spend just waiting for them to finish? What is the purpose of your contribution? To help that other person develop what they were saying, or to add your knowledge, your experience, your opinion?

4 About the activities

The activities in this book are meant to provide an experiential dimension to the learning which I hope will take place. After each chapter, there are some activities which focus specifically on classroom issues, and other activities which have a broader reference. All the activities are meant to function in the two areas of self-awareness and cooperative interaction which make up Cooperative Development.

The self-awareness work will not tell you about yourself, but it will give you a place to start thinking about yourself. In cooperative interaction, you will be able to develop those thoughts. The interactive techniques that you learn will also provide you with a working instrument for the development of your own teaching style.

The Speaker's space

I said in Chapter 2 that Cooperative Development is carried out in the roles of Speaker and Understander. The Speaker is the person who is going to work on his or her development during any given session.

In the last chapter, I said that Cooperative Development depends in part on the creation of space by the Understander for the Speaker. Because we are more used to conversations and discussions, in which we concentrate on making space for ourselves, this making space for someone else is often difficult to get used to. It can be useful if the Speaker and the Understander agree on some kind of a signal to be used in case the Understander encroaches on the Speaker's space. So if, as the Speaker, I feel that the Understander is not letting me follow my own ideas in my own way, but is more interested in introducing other ideas, I might just lift my hand slightly in an agreed way in order to say 'Hold off a little'.

The Observer

I have already introduced the roles of Speaker and Understander. The most important activities in terms of acquiring the interactive skills that underlie Cooperative Development are centred on the Speaker and the Understander. I have also added a third role, that of Observer.

The specific duties of the Observer are outlined with each activity, but the general function of the Observer is to give the Speaker and Understander feedback on what has happened from a third perspective. In so doing, the Observer will be learning to become analytical, and to listen especially for the way in which the Understander expresses the different moves that are being practised. As well as providing what I hope will be useful experiences in their own right, the activities as a set are meant to constitute a coherent course of learning which will make available to participants a new repertoire of interactive skills. Learning new skills always involves some practice, and can usually benefit from feedback. Hence, the Observer. The addition of the Observer, however, does highlight one issue that deserves more discussion: the 'artificiality' of the activities.

Artificiality

Firstly, the activities are fundamentally artificial, because Cooperative Development is meant to serve the internal motivation of Speakers to work on something important to themselves. As soon as I set a task for the Speaker, I have usurped the Speaker's essential independence. And yet, without some content, how can I present my ideas to you? What I have done is to provide initial tasks which I believe will be of interest to Speakers, and then indicate the outline of further tasks to which Speakers must provide the content.

Secondly, the activities are artificial because the Understander is asked to practise certain techniques from an initially very restricted repertoire. I see no way round this – the activities are meant to constitute a learning experience of which conscious practice is an important part. The activities will have been successful if Speakers and Understanders come to command the forms of cooperation which they can then employ towards their own ends.

Thirdly, the activities are artificial because they are observed. As I have already said, the purpose of using an Observer is to give feedback and thus enhance the learning process. Although there is undoubtedly a feeling of self-consciousness connected with being observed, most people usually become accustomed, and then quite oblivious, to the presence of the third person after a very short period of time. Furthermore, one group of teachers in Pakistan has reported that they have maintained the role of the Observer in their ongoing work, as they find that the richness of feedback enhances their learning and development.

The effectiveness of the Observer role can be helped by sensitive positioning. The Speaker and Understander should sit so that they feel comfortable and natural when speaking to each other. This is unlikely to be eyeball-to-eyeball. The best idea is to experiment and to talk about how different positions feel. When these two are comfortable, the Observer should take up a position that is clearly separate from them, but from which the Observer can keep a good eye on the Understander, as this role is more difficult to take on in the early stages of Cooperative Development.

While the role of the Observer is to comment on the interaction that takes place and to elicit retrospective comment from Speaker and Understander, these last two should also be engaged in ongoing commentary. This feature of Cooperative Development is worth introducing in its own right.

Commentaries

A running commentary on the interaction that is taking place between Speaker and Understander can frequently enhance that interaction. If one participant puts something particularly well, it is encouraging if the other points this out. Thus a Speaker might say, on hearing an Understander paraphrase the Speaker's idea: 'I really like the way you put that. That's exactly what I was trying to say'. Conversely, if one participant thinks that the interaction is going badly, it can also be helpful to say so. An Understander might say: 'I don't think that I'm getting this very clearly. I don't feel that I really understand what you're on about this morning at all'.

The quality of interaction may then become the topic of the interaction. This may appear self-defeating in the short term, but it is also a long term investment in better understanding. Such comments on the quality of communication frequently make the particular interaction work more efficiently, and they can certainly add to the overall development of empathy in continuing cooperation.

Open questions

Another useful generalisation that we can make at this stage concerns the questions that an Understander will want to ask in order to clarify what the Speaker is saying. Except in very clear cut cases, open questions which invite the speaker to say more are usually more effective than closed questions between fixed options, or questions which ask for a yes/no response. Closed questions tend to confront the Speaker with a choice between alternatives framed in the Understander's terms. So, if I ask, 'Could you tell me a bit more about why you use translation techniques in your classes?' I am more likely to hear what the Speaker really wants to say than if I ask, 'Do you use translation because the students find it easier?'

It is also worth noting that while a question such as the former of the above pair gives the Speaker the opportunity to expand and clarify, it does not give the Speaker confirmation of having been understood. That is the particular strength of the response described in Chapter 6 under *Reflecting*.

Silence

Finally, before we begin these activities in language towards action, it is worthwhile thinking about the importance of silence in interaction between two people working together. Nothing in this area is natural, everything is social, and must be thought of in its own cultural context.

The cultural background in which I grew up has little time for silence. Silence is more or less by definition a waste of time. It is also very embarrassing, and my culture has therefore developed a use of language called 'small talk', which is language-like behaviour meant not to communicate, but to fill up any silence that may occur when people are together.

Readers from a background which does not feel threatened by silence have an advantage here. For those readers from a background similar to my own, I want to put in two thoughts about silence that come out of my own culture.

Firstly, what does it tell you about your relationship with someone if you can sit in silence with that person and you both feel all right?

Secondly, the jazz musician Miles Davis was supposedly once criticised for not playing enough notes in his solos. He is said to have replied, 'The music is the space between the notes'.

I think that expression is important to development, but that expression sometimes needs silence in which to find itself. In the activities which follow, and in Cooperative Development generally, I do encourage you to allow for silence, to leave others and yourself the space to sit and think. Sometimes, perhaps, even the space just to sit.

Towards activity

Of course, readers can do whatever they wish with a book. I know that. And one good option is certainly to read the book through and see if you want to get involved in the activities.

Writers also have certain freedoms, so please excuse me if I remind you again that while the book's intellect is in the chapters, its heart is in the activities.

A rich understanding is brought about by articulating one's comprehension and experience in expression. I do hope that you have found a colleague or two to work with. Getting the most out of Cooperative Development depends on having colleagues you can rely on and trust. At the same time, Cooperative Development can help colleagues develop mutual trust and reliability.

PART 2
Exploration

The term **exploration** is being used here as a way of grouping together three interactive abilities that are central to Cooperative Development. They are **attending**, **reflecting**, and **focusing**. These abilities on the part of the Understander are meant to encourage the Speaker in the exploration of the topic that the Speaker has decided to work on.

5 Attending

As language teachers, we know that listening is not a passive process. We also know that we send out lots of messages to the people we are with, even when we are not actually speaking. We communicate by the way in which we sit or stand, by what we do with our hands, by the expression on our face, by the way we keep or break eye contact, by the little noises or exclamations we make while someone else is talking, and in a variety of other ways of which we are not usually conscious.

This unconscious process has been likened to having another self inside us who also speaks whether we do or not. When these two selves contradict each other, it is usually the 'other' who is telling the truth. I can lie to you, and I can control my face well enough to smile at you, but I may not notice that my fists are clenched and my ankles are locked under the chair. These signals give you a truer indication of my feelings than my smile or my words.

The complexity of both conscious and unconscious non-linguistic communication increases dramatically when people from different social and cultural backgrounds are involved. None of the behaviour that we grow up with is natural; it is all social and all learned, and what is polite in one culture may be offensive in another.

In my culture, it is essential for a listener to maintain eye contact with a speaker. If I am talking to you, I am perfectly free to look away for a while. But if, when I look back, you are also looking somewhere else, I assume that you are not interested in what I am saying. In other cultures, however, I know that relationships of age, gender and status play decisive roles in establishing the appropriacy of eye contact between speakers and listeners.

The ability that we want to develop is the ability to make someone feel well listened to. This ability relates particularly closely to the quality of non-judgmental respect that we have already talked about. We want to let the Speaker know that we are interested, that we are not making judgments, either positive or negative, and that we are making every effort to understand as fully as we can. Let me pick up a possible difficulty with the word *positive* here. We want to be positive in our commitment to understand, but we are not making positive/negative value judgments of what the Speaker has to say.

Nor is this meant to suggest that we should put on some sort of pantomime of exaggerated interest, full of *Oohs!* and *Aahs!* The actual suggestion is twofold. First, we should become more aware of how qualities such as interest, negative evaluation, and impatience are signalled. Secondly, we should learn to appear what we are and what we wish to be. If our aim is to encourage the Speaker, but we are sending out signals of aggression or boredom, we are unlikely to succeed.

If we are sending out such signals, we need to ask whether or not they are genuine. If we are feeling aggressive, this is something we can think about and talk about with the person we are working with. Making this aggressive attitude the topic of the cooperation is more likely to help future cooperation than trying to continue with something else when the Understander is in no shape to understand. In this case, we need to swap roles for a while at least; the Understander becomes the Speaker. If negativity is a recurring feature, we have to face up to the fact that none of us is compatible with everyone; we may be trying to cooperate with the wrong person.

If, on the other hand, we are unconsciously sending out signals which the Speaker interprets as signals of, say, boredom, we need to be more aware of those signals in order to remedy the situation. During a recent Cooperative Development workshop, I noticed that one Understander was staring intently at the floor while the Speaker, as far as I could tell, was becoming less and less sure of herself. I asked the Understander if she usually looked at someone who was speaking to her. 'No,' she said, 'but I was listening very carefully.' I then asked the Speaker if she had felt well listened to. 'No!' said the Speaker with some feeling, 'It was very difficult to keep going.' The point of the story is that the Understander was genuinely surprised to discover that her style of attending to what the Speaker had to say was having a negative effect on the Speaker's ability to express herself. As I have already said, this issue becomes particularly important in cross-cultural exchanges.

While it is relatively easy to see the danger of sending out negative signals, the danger of being too positive about what we hear also has to be countered. If the Understander sometimes nods and smiles and leans forward enthusiastically in approval, this is also evaluative behaviour which may well influence the Speaker. Furthermore, the withdrawal of this behaviour then takes on negative overtones of its own. One can see the same effect in any class where the teacher is reacting to student responses. If the first three responses are, 'Right!', 'Very good!' and 'Great!', then silence after the fourth response means that it is not acceptable.

Non-judgmental acceptance means exactly what it says: equal respect for what the Speaker has to say, regardless of the opinions of the Understander.

The starting point for each of us is to think about how we make a Speaker feel actively and supportively listened to. Then, as we do cooperate with a colleague, we can develop this ability in individual terms by talking about the quality of rapport that is building up. If you want to learn more about this area of body language, I have given some references in Chapter 15. What I want to do here is suggest some experiences that will help you start to think about your own body and its language.

Activities

The following activities involve silent but active listening. Please note that I am *not* suggesting that the Understander in Cooperative Development proper should remain silent. Simply, in these particular activities, we are focusing on non-linguistic responses.

Activity 5.1

☐ Most importantly, make an effort to observe consciously the way that people sit, stand and move their hands, arms and legs. Stereotypically, it is said that crossed arms and crossed legs represent barriers which we put up when we want to block something out. A hand to the mouth or chin suggests critical evaluation. Clenched fists signal frustration and possible aggression. When someone rubs the back of their neck, well, where do you think the expression 'a pain in the neck' comes from?

☐ So, observe yourself and others. My aim is to be myself, but to be as aware of myself as I can. There are more comments on this activity in Chapter 15.

Activity 5.2

☐ These are some illustrations taken from *Body Language* by Allan Pease. Discuss your interpretations of what you see. You can find an 'authorised version' of what is going on in Chapter 15.

5.2.a

5.2.b

5.2.c

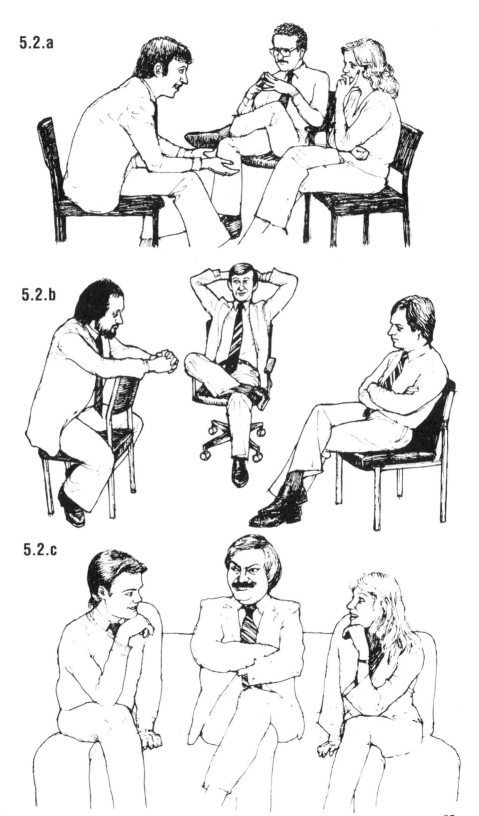

Activity 5.3

☐ What do you think makes a person feel well listened to, or not properly listened to? Make a list and compare yours with a colleague's.

Activity 5.4

☐ Form a group of three and choose one of the following topics for when you are Speaker. The Speaker talks for a couple of minutes on:

> One occasion in class when I felt really. . .
> annoyed, pleased with what I had done, relieved, embarrassed, frightened, amused, surprised, exhausted.

(Or supply any other adjective that you want to talk about.)

☐ Now decide on the initial roles of Speaker, Understander and Observer.

The Speaker tries to communicate the experience as well as he or she can.
The Understander tries to make the Speaker feel well listened to, but does not say anything.
The Observer sits apart and watches the Understander. The Observer makes notes on every move, gesture and expression the Understander makes.

☐ When the Speaker has finished, the Observer leads a feedback discussion.

Did the Speaker feel well listened to? How did the Understander feel? What movements did the Observer note down? Were the Speaker and Understander aware of them? Can you attach any significance to them?

☐ Now swap the roles around.

Activity 5.5

☐ Repeat Activity 4 on one of these topics:

> One occasion when I was lost.
> One occasion when I lost something important to me.
> One occasion when someone I know was lost.

☐ This time, the Understander makes no effort to make the Speaker feel well listened to. As Understander, lean back, cross your arms, look at the ceiling. Think of impatience, think of boredom, think of frustration and let your body show it while keeping a neutral expression on your face.

☐ When the Speaker has finished, the Observer leads a discussion as before: Did the Speaker feel well listened to? How did the Understander feel? What movements did the Observer note down? Were Speaker and Understander aware of them? Can you attach any significance to them?

Activity 5.6

One of the surest signs of fellow feeling or affinity between two people is when they unconsciously 'mirror' each other's physical position, so that one looks like a reflection of the other. You can see this in one of the illustrations above. We can also use mirroring in a conscious activity:

☐ **A** leads by sitting with eyes closed and thinking in detail about some meaningful past event as a teacher or a student which evokes memories of strong feelings and/or of physical activity. Examples might be:

Reliving an interview for a job I didn't get.
Conducting a group of EFL beginners singing 'Yellow Submarine' at an end-of-term party.

These are my own examples. The point is that the more involved **A** becomes, the better for the activity.

☐ **B** sits opposite **A** and mirrors **A**'s facial expression, posture and body movement as closely and exactly as possible. **A** keeps the eyes closed so as to spare both **A** and **B** any embarrassment.

☐ When **A** has finished, **B** comments on what happened. A third person, acting as Observer, can also be useful here. There are further comments on this activity in Chapter 15.

6 Reflecting

The active Understander

Some of your discussion regarding the activities at the end of the last chapter might have raised the issue of whether the Understander is active or passive. Is the Understander just supposed to sit and listen?

Certainly not. The purpose of the last chapter was to highlight the importance of making a Speaker feel well listened to. This chapter and subsequent ones will give the Understander an ever more active role. But let's make sure we don't confuse this active role with involvement in a conversation or a discussion.

In a conversation or a discussion, you take part by putting forward your own opinion, referring to your own experience, arguing your own case. You may have felt a desire to do this during the activities at the end of Chapter 5. If you kept to the rules, as Understander, you may have felt a little frustration that you were not supposed to add your own contributions. After the activities, in fact, you may have gone back to some of the things that were said by the Speaker and taken part in a more usual conversational exchange about them by making your own comments and recalling experiences of your own. In this way, you released the frustration built up by your having taken on the role of Understander.

This frustration at not being able to make your usual conversational contribution is, however, at the heart of being an Understander. I hope that your feeling of frustration will grow as you get involved in more activities as Understander. I hope that you will then start to gain satisfaction from not releasing this frustration in a flow of your own opinions and interpretations. The frustration is itself a source of energy.

This energy can be put at the service of Speakers in order to help them develop their own opinions, interpretations and plans. Exactly how this can be done is the business of this book, as the Understander takes on an ever more active role which does not take up the developmental space of the Speaker.

The next step in the building of that role is a crucial one. If, as Understander, you can develop the ability to *reflect*, then everything else follows.

Reflecting

As should now be clear, the central idea of teacher development is that it is self-development. I take responsibility for deciding which aspect of my teaching I want to extend or to abandon. In order to make the necessary evaluation of my present position, I need help in seeing it clearly.

One way in which a colleague can help me is by listening actively and sympathetically to what I have to say. A further method of helping me is when my colleague acts as a mirror in order to reflect back my ideas in such a way that I can get a clear view of them.

Imagine that the Speaker is talking about reading classes with a particular group of students. The Understander might reflect what the Speaker has said like this:

a

> Let me see if I've got this right. You think that it's really important to insist that the students read the reading passage before they come to class. What's going wrong at the moment is that a number of them aren't doing so, and you want to do something about that.

I used the metaphor of a mirror to describe reflecting. I hope that that makes the idea of reflecting clear. However, a mirror is hard and cold, and I want to get rid of that part of the metaphor. Reflecting also has to catch the attitude and emotion of the Speaker, because the unspoken emotion might turn out to be more important that the plain facts. So, in the same situation as I have just referred to, the Understander might continue:

b

> You're pretty fed up about these students who don't do the reading you ask them to. You feel that you're doing your best, and they're getting in the way of your teaching as well as you can. It's unfair, because they're spoiling the class for everybody.

So, the mirror has to be a warm, human mirror. By the same token, reflecting has some of the characteristics of a tape recorder, but it has to be a thoughtful, selective tape recorder. What I mean by this is that it is important to reflect what the Speaker has said in the Speaker's own terms.

In some cases, this might involve using the same words that the Speaker used. In other cases, a paraphrase might be the most natural and effective way of showing the meanings that have been understood. In this latter case, it's important to use words and expressions that are appropriate to the Speaker's perspective and ways of expression. So, the Understander tries to use technical terminology or slang to the same extent that the Speaker does, otherwise the use of language might appear to move the exchange out of the Speaker's frame of reference and into the Understander's. An intentionally exaggerated example of this might be:

c

SPEAKER: I get this feeling that at least some of the students have got a lot more English in them than I'm getting out.

UNDERSTANDER: So, if I'm understanding you properly, you sense a latent tendency in a proportion of the participants to underperform their actual communicative competence.

In this exchange, the Understander is taking the Speaker's experience and expressing it in terms far removed from the Speaker's own. It is unlikely that the Speaker will recognise the original statement in this paraphrase.

Also unwanted is any element of interpretation or explanation by the Understander:

d

SPEAKER: I find correction a bit of a bother with this class. There are some very competitive students in there who hate to be corrected.

UNDERSTANDER: When you say they hate to be corrected, do you mean corrected by you, or are you including self-correction and peer correction in that?

Here, the Understander has supplied an analytical framework for the Speaker to fit his or her experience into. It may be a good analytical framework, but that is not the point. No one will ever know the direction that the Speaker's expression of experience would have taken if the Understander had said something like:

e

UNDERSTANDER: So there's a negative reaction to correction. And you find this important, yes?

In other words, the Understander needs to say: 'This is what I am hearing. This is what I have understood. Have I got it right?'

At its simplest, reflecting works as a comprehension check. If you can reflect to me the ideas I am trying to get across, in terms that I recognise as either my own or appropriate to my ideas, and if you can also show me the feelings that I have about these ideas, then you know that you are understanding me successfully. At the same time, I know that you are really with me, and I am encouraged to go on.

Clearly, the ability to reflect accurately is thus closely associated with the attitudinal concept of empathy. Successful reflection helps establish and extend an empathetic relationship, and this is its main, long term importance. More immediately, reflection has another, very significant function.

When I see someone making every effort to understand my position, I listen very carefully to what they have to say. I look very closely at the image that they reflect to me. It may be that all is well with that image, that I like what I see, and we can continue. But all may not be well. Either at that moment, or later on, I may start to wonder if I am content with the image that I saw.

The Speaker in the example a/b above, for instance, may start to think that there are better places to expend energy than in thinking of ways to force students to read passages before class. The Speaker may think that carrying feelings of resentment from class to class is as much of a problem as the behaviour of the students. When the Speaker starts to think like this, there is the possibility of development as we have been using the term - creative growth coming out of the self.

What the Understander must not do – because it would be dishonest – is to reflect an idea with the thought or implication that this is something which the Speaker should reconsider. Evaluation must come from the Speaker. At this point, exploration begins to develop a potential for discovery.

In the early stages, Understanders are sometimes embarrassed by the act of reflecting. They feel silly repeating what someone has just said, or they think that it is insulting to the Speaker. In part, this feeling has to do with the timing of when one reflects. Nothing has significance if it is done mechanically. If reflection is used as a genuine comprehension check, when the Understander wants to be sure of not misunderstanding something, or losing track, then there should be no embarrassment.

After some experience as an Understander, most people come to realise that reflection is not a trivial act. It is difficult to reflect accurately and empathetically, but reflection is of great help to the Speaker, and to the relationship on which Cooperative Development is based. The following exercises are intended to begin that experience.

Activities

Activity 6.1

☐ How might you reflect the following statements? Read each statement carefully, look up from the page, and reflect. Even if you are alone, it's important that you actually speak and not just think what you would say. Check your attempts with a colleague and talk carefully about the words that you choose, especially those that refer to emotions. If you have a tape recorder, recording your reflections might help the discussion.

- 'I'm fed up with people telling me to use group work. The students don't learn anything and they just sit and talk in their own language until the teacher gets to their group. I don't really blame them, either. I'd do the same.'

- 'The best part of my lessons is always when I get them in groups and they work on something together, you know, a problem to solve. It's really magic how involved they get and they're always asking how to say different things they can't say in English.'

- 'I'm dreading the start of next term. Another group of students, the same book, the same mistakes to correct, the same exams, the same excuses, and no end to it.'

- 'Last year's students said they would have liked more project work, so that's what I'm going to try. Of course, this year's lot might be just the opposite, but you've got to start somewhere, haven't you? I'm scared to death really, 'cause I didn't think last year's projects went that well and I haven't had time to prepare anything brilliant.'

- 'There has to be a way to contextualise intonation practice more effectively in meaningful interaction. I mean, I'm not prepared to leave intonation to some chance of acquisition, but I don't want us to spend our time on some sort of behaviourist chanting, either.'

Activity 6.2

☐ The Understander will frequently have to interrupt the Speaker in order to reflect. You may find it useful to think about the kind of phrase which you could use in order to make this interruption. How might you extend this list with expressions that you feel comfortable with?
- Just a minute, let me see if I've got this right. . . .
- OK, what I hear you saying is this. . . .
- Can I just check something with you? . . .
- So, if I'm understanding you properly, . . .
- Right, so it looks like this. . . .

Activity 6.3

☐ Now go back to Activity 5.4 again using the roles of the Speaker, the Understander and the Observer.

☐ This time, the Understander listens actively to what the Speaker has to say, and then reflects it to the Speaker, trying also to make explicit any emotional or attitudinal aspects that the Understander thinks are present.

☐ The Observer again looks out for body language and also listens carefully to the reflecting. Is it accurate? Is it empathetic? How did the Speaker feel? How about the Understander? These questions form the basis of the feedback discussion.

Activity 6.4

Individual task

☐ Read the following story.

Lima was a student teacher in her final year. Her father had brought her up alone after her mother's death and, although very poor, he had made every sacrifice in order to provide for her education.

Lima had lots of fun at college, but did very little work. When the time came, it was clearly going to be impossible for her to pass the final examinations. Without her teaching certificate, she would not be able to get any kind of job.

She asked her tutor what she should do. This woman said that it was too late to think about such things now and that Lima should have worked harder. Lima asked another lecturer. He said that he would give her the examination questions if she would go to bed with him. She did so, and passed the examinations.

However, Lima also became pregnant. When her father found out, he threw her out of the house and refused to have anything more to do with her.

Now homeless, penniless and expecting a baby, Lima met a much older man who was a widower with three children. He said that he would be prepared to marry her as long as she stayed at home and looked after his house and children.

☐ Now number the characters from 1 to 5 according to how easy you find it to sympathise with their actions. Number 1 is the character with whom you can most easily sympathise. *Do not talk about your sequence with anyone.*

Lima   Father   Tutor   Lecturer   Widower

Group task

☐ Sit in a group of three and decide who will be Speaker, Understander and Observer. Carry out the following task:

☐ *The Speaker*: Talk briefly through your numbering of the characters in the story, giving reasons for this sequence and any comments on the task. Do not speak for more than five minutes.

☐ *The Understander*: Listen actively. Make the Speaker feel listened to. Reflect the Speaker's sequencing of the characters and the reasoning behind it, also any feelings the Speaker had while carrying out the task. You can either wait until the Speaker has finished before reflecting, or come in while the Speaker is talking. The purposes of Reflecting are:

  • to check comprehension and communication of ideas and feelings;

  • to demonstrate respect and increase empathy;

  • to provide a basis for development of the Speaker's ideas.

☐ *The Observer*: Pay particular attention to the Understander, noting any non-linguistic communication. Also pay special attention to the Understander's attempts to reflect, noting anything that seems particularly successful or unsuccessful. Remember, it should not be possible for you to tell what the Understander thinks about the Speaker's sequencing and reasons for that sequencing.

☐ After not more than ten minutes, lead a feedback session, contributing the above information and asking for the reactions and contributions of Speaker and Understander. The following questions are central:

  • Did the Speaker feel 'understood', in the sense that we are using the term?

  • Did the Speaker understand his or her own ideas better after having expressed them?

  • Did the Speaker's ideas develop at all as they were being expressed?

  • What were the Speaker's reactions to the Understander, especially with reference to reflecting?

  • How did the Understander feel while trying to reflect without revealing his or her own opinions (i.e. with respect and empathy)?

  • How does the Speaker feel about not having heard the opinions of the Understander and Observer?

  There are further comments on this activity in Chapter 15.

7 Focusing

Any conversation about teaching, whether in general terms or concerning an aspect of an observed lesson, tends to go on for a long time and cover a wide variety of topics. The purpose of Cooperative Development is to move towards action, and talk therefore needs to be *focused*.

After a period involving attending and reflection, the Understander can often help the Speaker work on the Speaker's understanding of experience by focusing the Speaker's attempts at expression. Focusing can either be elicited by the Understander from the Speaker, or done directly by the Understander.

Let us take the example of a reading lesson which the Understander has observed. Let us assume that the Speaker asked the Understander to concentrate on the work that was done before the students actually started on the reading passage itself.

Now, while talking about this stage of the lesson, the Speaker might refer to what happened during the warm-up, to attempts to elicit topic knowledge from the class, to the introduction of important new words, and to the setting of pre-text questions. At this point, the Understander might say:

> Right. From what you've covered so far, what's the most interesting part for you? Is there something there you would like to concentrate on?

This asks the Speaker to think back and choose a *focus* for further work. The Speaker, of course, retains the right not to accept this focusing and may wish to carry on talking about other topics. The role of the Understander is to continue to furnish the Speaker with opportunities to pursue some point that the Speaker has raised in greater depth, and move towards action.

Between people who are used to cooperating, and who have developed a feeling of trust and empathy, the Understander might want to say something like:

> Shall we go back to when you were talking about eliciting vocab from the students? Do you want to say some more about that?

Here, the Understander is trying to provide a direct focus because of the impression that the Speaker's own interests and purposes can best be served in this way. Perhaps there was an impression that the Speaker could have said more about this aspect of the topic but decided at the time to move on. If we look back at example **d** in the last chapter, the Understander might have responded like this:

SPEAKER: I find correction a bit of a bother with this class. There are some very competitive students in there who hate to be corrected.

UNDERSTANDER: I hear you say that some of the students really dislike being corrected. Do you want to talk some more about correction?

However, what the Understander must not do is try to hijack the Speaker's development towards the Understander's interests and purposes. Nor must the Understander lead the Speaker to focus on what the Understander believes the Speaker 'would be well advised to' focus on. As well as depending on empathy, the ability to focus the Speaker's discourse thus makes direct demands on the Understander's honesty in the interaction.

During the early stages of cooperation, it is probably more useful for the Understander to concentrate on *eliciting* a focus, rather than suggesting one. In this way, the Understander will build up an image of how the Speaker most naturally finds a focus. This, in turn, will help the Understander become more empathetic with this Speaker.

I have stressed the link between finding a focus and deciding on action. Because of this strong connection, we shall return to the area of focusing in Chapter 11, when we work on setting action goals. For the time being, however, let us pursue the idea of focusing our ideas at increasing depth.

Most teachers, I think, have had groups of learners which they look back on with particular warmth. Think back, either as teacher or student, to a class that you regularly enjoyed being in. Is there one class that you have particularly warm memories of? Personally, I think back to the second year group (56 students) of 1982/83 at the Foreign Languages Education Department, Istanbul University. If you can place such a group of students in your own life, please join me in the following exercise:

1 Write down the class that you think of and draw two circles round it:

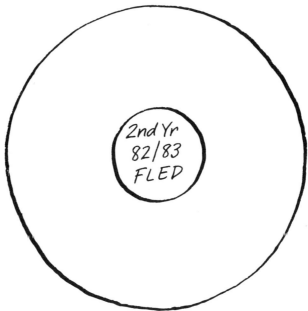

2 Divide the space between the circles into four segments. In each segment write down something that was good about that class, some element that contributed to the good feeling that you have. This is how my circles look:

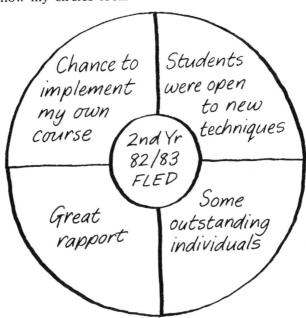

3 Now take one of those elements and put it at the centre of a focusing circle. Then ask yourself, 'What was so good about this? Why did I find this so important?' Put your responses around the segments of the focusing circle. Mine now looks like this:

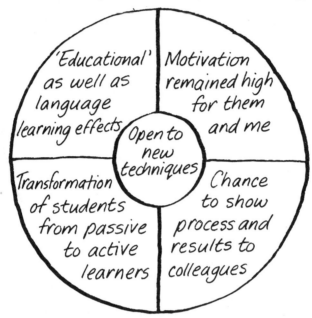

4 Repeat the previous stage:

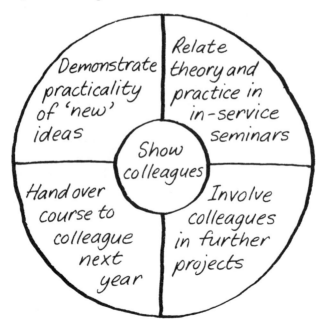

As I focus closer and explore more deeply one aspect of the topic, I discover elements in it that I was simply not aware of. I can only hope that you believe me when I tell you that I had not realised until I wrote this down that a part of my enjoyment of that particular class arose from the fact that I could use my success with it to encourage my colleagues to experiment more freely with the syllabus and the teaching styles that they had been using up till that time.

This is exactly in the spirit of Cooperative Development: as we explore our ideas, we awaken a potential for discovery. We shall move more into this area of discovery in Part 3 of the book. But first, let me invite you to work on the following activities.

Activities

Activity 7.1

☐ Choose one of the following topics and put it at the centre of a focusing circle:

testing	*my colleagues*
a textbook	*parents*
teaching listening	*marking*

☐ Now work with a partner or, even better, two partners. The Speaker should work on the chosen topic through at least two rounds of the focusing exercise as described above. While doing this, the Speaker should keep up a running commentary on what is being chosen to go into the segments of the circle.
☐ As each segment is filled in, the Understander reflects what the Speaker has said in order to check communication. When all four segments are filled, the Understander invites the Speaker to focus on one of them, thus taking the Speaker into the next stage of the process.
☐ A third person, if available, will take on the role of Observer and lead the feedback discussion when the Speaker wants to stop.

Activity 7.2

☐ It might be useful for you to think of some phrases that you can use when you want to help someone find a focus. How could you extend this list?
- Is there anything we've covered so far that you'd like to go back to?
- Is there anything in what you've said that you'd like to focus on?
- OK, do you want to work a bit deeper into any of this?
- Right, do you want to stop and go further into that?

Activity 7.3

☐ Repeat the first activity above, using a topic of your own. Be sure also that you have a chance at some stage to experience the activity in more than one role, that is as the Speaker, the Understander and perhaps as Observer.

Activity 7.4

☐ This time, let the Speaker choose a topic to talk about without using the circles.

☐ The Understander should reflect and attempt to help the Speaker find a focus. Remember, the purposes of focusing are to help Speakers:

   get beyond a superficial level of talk;

   select something from what they have already said in order to develop their ideas in more detail;

   deal with specifics as part of a move towards action.

Activity 7.5

Individual task

☐ Complete the following questionnaire. It asks you to make judgments about your position at work. If you don't have a job at the moment, you can relate the questions to a previous job. If you have never worked, you may be able to relate the items to your position as a student, or to your position in some other organisation. Of course, questionnaire items never fit anyone exactly. Your purpose should be to use the questionnaire to give you some structured information about your current role which you can then use as the basis for focusing further thought towards action.

☐ What you have to do is to choose for each item the response which comes closest to describing your situation. Please circle only one response for each item.

Role Effectiveness Profile

1 **a** My role is very important in this institution. I feel central here.
   b I am doing useful and fairly important work here.
   c Very little importance is given to my work; I feel peripheral here.

2 **a** My training and expertise are not fully used in my present role.
   b My training and knowledge are not used in my present role.
   c I am able to use my knowledge and training very well here.

3 **a** I have little freedom in my role; I just do what I am told.
   b I operate inside the framework that is given to me.
   c I can take the initiative and act on my own in my role.

4 **a** I am doing normal, routine work in my role.
   b In my role, I am able to use my creativity and do new things.
   c I have no time for creative work in my role.

5 **a** No one responds to my ideas or suggestions.
   b I work very closely with some other colleagues.
   c I am alone in my role and have almost no one to consult.

6 **a** When I need some help, none is available.
   b Whenever things aren't going well, others help me.
   c I get very hostile responses when I ask for help.

7 **a** I do not have the opportunity to contribute to society in my role.
   b The work that I do is likely to benefit society in general.
   c I have the opportunity to have some effect on society.

8 **a** I make some contribution to decisions here.
   b I have no power here.
   c My advice is accepted by my seniors.

9 **a** Some of what I do contributes to my learning.
   b I am slowly forgetting all that I learned in my training.
   c I have great opportunities for professional growth here.

10 **a** I dislike being bothered with problems.
   b When someone brings a problem to me, I like to help find a
      solution.
   c If people bring up problems, I refer them to the relevant person.

11 **a** I feel I'm at the heart of what is going on here.
  b I feel my work is quite valuable to the institution.
  c My role is not at all essential here, I'm out on the fringe.

12 **a** I do not enjoy my role.
  b I enjoy my role very much.
  c I enjoy some parts of my role and not others.

13 **a** I have little freedom in my role.
  b I have a great deal of freedom to act on my own decisions.
  c I have some freedom of action in my role.

14 **a** I do a good job according to a schedule already decided.
  b I am able to innovate and change things around.
  c I have no opportunity to be creative or try anything new.

15 **a** Other people in the institution see my role as significant.
  b I am a member of a committee or group working on something.
  c I do not work on any committees or groups.

16 **a** Hostility rather than cooperation is evident here.
  b I experience enough mutual help here.
  c People here tend to operate alone.

17 **a** I make a fair contribution to the work of our institution.
  b In my role, I am able to serve society at large.
  c I wish I could do something useful for more people.

18 **a** I am able to influence relevant decisions.
  b I am sometimes consulted on important matters.
  c I have no chance to make any independent decisions.

19 **a** I learn a great deal in my role.
  b I sometimes learn new things in my role.
  c I am involved in routine or unrelated activities and have learned nothing.

20 **a** When people bring me problems. I tend to ask them to work them out themselves.
  b I dislike being bothered with interpersonal conflict.
  c I enjoy solving problems related to my work.

☐ On the scoring key, circle the number corresponding to your response to each of the twenty items. Then, look along the various dimensions, where you will see that each dimension has two questions attached to it. For each dimension, you have a maximum score of +4, and a minimum of –2. Find your own score for each dimension. Finally, calculate your general Role effectiveness index.

Scoring Key

dimension	item	responses a	responses b	responses c	item	responses a	responses b	responses c	dimension score
Centrality	1	+2	+1	–1	11	+2	+1	–1	. . . . .
Integration	2	+1	–1	+2	12	–1	+2	+1	. . . . .
Initiative	3	–1	+1	+2	13	–1	+2	+1	. . . . .
Creativity	4	+1	+2	–1	14	+1	+2	–1	. . . . .
Connections	5	–1	+2	+1	15	+2	+1	–1	. . . . .
Help	6	+1	+2	–1	16	–1	+2	+1	. . . . .
Wider value	7	–1	+2	+1	17	+1	+2	–1	. . . . .
Influence	8	+1	–1	+2	18	+2	+1	–1	. . . . .
Development	9	+1	–1	+2	19	+2	+1	–1	. . . . .
Problems	10	–1	+2	+1	20	+1	–1	+2	. . . . .

Total . . . .

$$\text{Role effectiveness index} = \frac{\text{Total score} + 20}{60} \times 100 = \%$$

Group task

☐ *The Speaker*: Begin by talking about your feelings on your role effectiveness in general after completing the questionnaire. Then, when the Understander invites you to focus, choose one of the dimensions on which you have your lowest score. Talk about why you think your score is so low. Is it because this dimension is not important to you? If it is important, explore the question: *Is my score here so low despite all my efforts, or could I do more in this area?*

☐ *The Understander*: Listen actively and reflect as the Speaker works on his or her general role effectiveness. Then invite the Speaker to focus. When the Speaker has focused on one particular dimension, see if there is a still closer focus to be found within that dimension.

□ *The Observer*: Watch and listen carefully, especially to the Understander's attempts to reflect and focus. Then give feedback and help the Speaker and the Understander talk about their feelings during the exercise. Central questions are:
- Did the Speaker feel well listened to?
- Did the Speaker discover anything new while exploring his or her ideas?
- Did the Understander succeed in helping the Speaker without introducing the Understander's ideas and experiences?
- Did the Understander feel frustrated by the need not to talk about him or herself?
- Did the Understander enjoy the discipline of working to give the Speaker space to develop?

PART 3
Discovery

On the way towards action, the purpose of exploration is **discovery**. Speaker and Understander cooperate to discover inside the Speaker's focus a basis for the Speaker's future action.

We are going to look at three moves available to the Understander at this stage: **thematising, challenging** and **disclosing**. All three involve linking ideas which are initially separate. These moves are more overtly active and interventionist than the abilities we looked at earlier. Consequently, they make an increased demand on the Understander's qualities of respect, empathy and honesty.

8 Thematising

As we have noted, the Speaker may range over a variety of topics on the way to formulating a focus for action. Also when a focus has been found, a variety of aspects may well be treated.

On some occasions, the Speaker will make separate points which the Understander may think are connected, or at least related, to each other. When this happens, the Understander can bring this possible relationship to the attention of the Speaker.

For example, the Speaker might be talking about a class that is not going particularly well. In describing the students the Speaker may say at one point:

> They do good grammar exercises, but they don't have anything to say for themselves when they write.

Later, the Speaker may say:

> They're not too good at reading. They're forever asking what all the words mean.

The dialogue might continue as follows:

UNDERSTANDER: On that last point, I hear you saying that there are usually quite a few words they don't know. Is that right?

SPEAKER: Yes, I tell them to read on, but it doesn't work.

UNDERSTANDER: Well, you said a while back that they don't have anything to say when they write. Do you think that there's a connection between the two points?

The Understander has brought together two statements made by the Speaker in order to see if there is any thematic relationship between them. Various possibilities may follow.

Firstly, the Speaker may deny any relationship, in which case none exists, at least for the time being. In explaining why there is no connection, the Speaker will explore the possibility, and clarify his or her position while consolidating the channel of communication. The Speaker may come back to think about this point later. The Speaker may even see a relationship later and think of it as an original idea, which is what it will be.

Secondly, the Speaker may recognise the relation as something well known, but perhaps insignificant. As with the first possibility, there may be later developments, but for the time being the major function is clarifying communication.

Thirdly, the Speaker may acknowledge a connection that he or she had not thought of before. This connection may provide a good basis for development. There does not have to be a rush to hypothesis here, nor should the Understander provide a thematic link. Indeed, sometimes the Understander might want to back an intuitive hunch without seeing a definite link. At other times the thematising might be motivated by a particular idea. In either case, the Understander offers a potential link and leaves it at that. The Speaker should take the time to consider possible connections.

Based on the example above, perhaps a lack of vocabulary was the link that the Understander saw between the students' boring essays and their reading difficulties. So, the Understander might have wanted to suggest that the Speaker spend more time on vocabulary enrichment exercises. But the Understander does not make any such suggestion.

The Speaker, however, working on the intuition that there may be a connection between the reading and writing problems, might think, or say:

> Yes, maybe there is a connection. Those reading passages aren't really about anything that the students are interested in or know anything about, so they don't have the vocabulary. Same with the essay titles – there's nothing in them that the students can really relate to their lives outside school. Maybe if I tried some new titles and looked for passages that related to those topics, that would get them involved. Of course, we'd have to get back to the old passages at some stage because of the exam, but . . .

So now the Speaker may get involved in using topics and activities which invite more personal involvement on behalf of the learners, without necessarily concentrating overtly on vocabulary enrichment.

The purpose of the work that we are describing here is to encourage the Speaker's development in terms of thought and action. The Understander holds back with advice and suggestions because these will influence the Speaker's ideas. The Speaker needs space to grow into. There may be some frustration involved in that space, as well as time and silence, but these are necessary ingredients of development.

As long as two people have agreed on this mode of interaction in a sense of respect, empathy and honesty, the frustration is a positive sign of a point for development. Just as the Understander does not come forward with advice and suggestions, the Speaker does not ask for them – they are not what the Understander is there to provide.

If there is no way forward on a particular topic at a particular time, this can be noted for further individual work later and the interaction can continue in a different direction.

The particular ability that we have looked at in this chapter is *thematising*. I hope that the concept is clear, and I encourage you to build up some experiential understanding through the following activities.

Activities

Activity 8.1

Individual task

☐ Take a sheet of paper and draw a line down the middle. On the left hand side, make a list of activities *outside teaching* that you are good at, or that you enjoy, or both. What are the activities that give you the feeling: 'This is me at my best'? Include them in the list. This is private information. You will have the opportunity to tell someone about these things if you want to, but you will be able to choose what you mention and what you don't. Please do this before you read on.

☐ Look down the list again. Ask yourself, in each case, 'What are the skills, or qualities, or abilities that I bring to each of these activities? What is it that gives me the sense of enjoyment or of satisfaction that I find in them?'

☐ Now, on the right hand side of the paper, opposite the relevant activities, make a list of these qualities, abilities and skills, and of the sources of enjoyment and satisfaction that you experience outside teaching.

Group task

☐ Sit in a group of three and decide who will be Speaker, Understander and Observer. Carry out the following task:

☐ *The Speaker*: Your aim is to increase your awareness of the strengths and abilities that you have, to recognise how you use them in your teaching, and perhaps to discover a greater potential for enjoyment and for feeling at your best in your work.

Talk briefly through a selection of the non-teaching activities that you have listed and the skills that they entail. Try to discover possible connections with your teaching. Where and how do you use these abilities in your teaching? When, in your teaching, do you enjoy yourself? When do you feel, 'This is me at my best'? Could you use your strengths more often? Could you get more enjoyment and feel at your best more often?

☐ *The Understander*: Listen actively. Make the Speaker feel listened to. Reflect the Speaker's ideas and feelings where appropriate. Help the Speaker find a focus. Listen particularly for any possible connections which the Speaker does not make, and offer these for comment.

Remember, the purposes of thematising are:

- to check comprehension and communication of ideas and feelings;
- to give the Speaker a chance to make previously unseen connections between ideas;
- to provide a basis for possible development by the Speaker.

☐ *The Observer*: Pay particular attention to the Understander, noting any non-linguistic communication. Pay special attention to the Understander's attempts to thematise, noting anything that seems particularly successful or unsuccessful.

☐ After not more than fifteen minutes, the Observer leads a feedback session, contributing the above information and asking for the reactions and contributions of Speaker and Understander. Important questions are:
- Did the Speaker feel 'understood', in our sense of the term?
- Did the Speaker's awareness of his or her strengths and abilities increase?
- Did the Speaker find the attempts at thematising useful?
- How did the Understander feel while trying to thematise without making his or her own connections explicit (i.e. with respect and empathy)?
- How did the Speaker feel about not hearing the Understander's opinions?

Activity 8.2

Individual task

☐ You need two blank sheets of paper and something to write with. Get ready to write on one sheet. Are you ready? If you're not, please don't read on.

☐ Are you ready now? As quickly as you can, without giving too much thought to it, write down *at least* twelve adjectives that describe you. This is private; you won't be asked to share anything you don't want to. Please do that now. When you've finished, put that sheet of paper away and out of sight.

☐ On the opposite page you'll find a pattern. At the centre of the pattern is a dot. When you've finished reading these instructions, (but not before!) please look at the page and concentrate your gaze on the dot at the centre of the pattern.

☐ First of all, make sure you are sitting comfortably. It will probably help if you put both feet flat on the floor. Straighten your back so that your shoulders are above your hips. Take a deep breath. And let it out. And another breath. And out. Try to keep your breathing deep and regular.

☐ When you look at the page and begin to concentrate on the dot at the centre of the pattern, try to clear your mind of thoughts. This is more or less impossible, but you can try. When you realise you are thinking about something, just gently ease that thought out of your mind and think about your breathing, keeping it deep and regular, and concentrate on the dot at the centre of the pattern. When you realise that you are thinking about something else, do the same thing again.

• Try to clear your mind.
• You simply concentrate your vision on the dot at the centre of the pattern.
• Check the time now.
• Continue the activity for *at least* five minutes and not more than ten.
• Sit in a relaxed way so that you can look at the pattern for five to ten minutes without getting uncomfortable.
• Keep your breathing deep and regular.
• If you find that you need to think about something, think about your breathing.
• As much as you can, though, clear your mind of thoughts.
• When thoughts come into your consciousness, just recognise that they are there and ease them out of your mind.
• Keep your eyes focused on the dot at the centre of the pattern.

☐ Please look at the opposite page and begin.

☐ If you have been concentrating on the pattern for up to the last ten minutes, you probably won't want to do anything very quickly. So, slowly, pick up your pen and the empty sheet of paper. Now move your pen to the hand that you do not normally write with. If you are right handed, take the pen in your left hand. On the empty sheet of paper, as quickly as you can and without thinking about it too much, write down at least twelve adjectives that describe you. Don't worry about the quality of the writing, only you have to be able to read it. Please do that now.

Group task

☐ Form a group of three and decide who will be the Speaker, the Understander and the Observer. Carry out the following task:

☐ *The Speaker*: You have a choice of aims, or you can attempt both. Both give you a chance to talk a little about yourself in an unfamiliar situation.

One possibility is simply to explore the experience of sitting quietly and concentrating on the pattern. What was it like? What happened? How did you feel? How do you feel now? Are there any comments you want to make? Would you like to try the experience again?

Another possibility would be to spend a little time looking at the two lists of adjectives that you made. Talk about those items in each list that you feel happy to talk about. Do you notice any overall similarity between the items in each single list? Do you notice any overall difference between the items in the two separate lists? If there is any general difference between the two lists, how would you describe that difference?

☐ *The Understander*: Your purpose, as ever, is to help the Speaker develop his or her ideas. You should be using the skills of attending, reflecting and focusing, as they seem appropriate. Listen especially for an opportunity to thematise.

☐ *The Observer*: I hope that the Observer's role is now clear. Please refer to the suggestions in the previous activity for guidelines.

☐ In Chapter 15, I have added a few comments on where this activity comes from and the thinking behind it. I do encourage you to carry out the activity before reading any more about it.

9 Challenging

Let us begin with a negative definition. Challenging is *not* to be understood in its everyday, interpersonal sense of: *You state your opinion and I challenge you to prove it*, or *I challenge you with my opinion*. I hope that this does not come as a surprise.

Challenging is closely connected to thematising. It is like the other side of the same coin. That is to say, you may hear me make two statements and, as Understander, you may find it difficult to see how I can maintain both at the same time. As Understander, you present me with these two statements and ask me to reconcile them. In other words, the challenge comes from the Understander, but only in terms of the coherence of the Speaker's own views. The Understander is still trying to work inside the Speaker's frame of reference.

For instance, I might be talking about how I teach vocabulary. I might say how I detest the use of word-lists, what a waste of time they are, and how I strongly discourage students from using them. Later on, I might mention the importance of catering for different learning styles among the learners. An Understander might say:

> 'I hear you say that it's important to allow for different ways that
> the students have of learning. How does that match up with
> what you were saying earlier about discouraging word-lists?'

So now, as the Speaker, I have to see how these two opinions of mine fit together. Do I really believe that different learners will have different ways of learning and that learners should be encouraged to choose ways that suit them best? If so, mustn't I accept that some learners will want to use word-lists? Or do I believe that, while there is a wide variety of useful learning strategies, some strategies – such as using word-lists – are never of any use and should be discouraged?

If I can reconcile these two statements to my own satisfaction, then the challenge was useful in that it clarified for both of us (Speaker and Understander) exactly what I think. Remember, as the Speaker, I do not have to satisfy the Understander, I have to satisfy myself. Having made the challenge, the Understander is not there to argue, but to understand. Reflecting is often appropriate here for the Understander.

If I cannot reconcile the two positions then, as Speaker, I have some work to do on what it is I actually believe and how that is to affect my teaching. This is a basis for development. Also, we have to remember that no matter how the position is left now, I may return to these thoughts later on my own.

All the points made in the discussion of thematising about space, time, silence, frustration and the shift to another topic are relevant again here.

Challenging is the most threatening move that we have looked at. It would be all too easy to score points by implying that a Speaker is being 'illogical' or 'incoherent'. To do this would be to behave as if in a discussion, where we take the other person's utterances to be a finished product which is sent out into the conversational arena to look after itself. In Cooperative Development, the Understander is trying to support the Speaker's process of developing ideas: there is as yet no logical or illogical, no coherent or incoherent. The challenge must be a real question as to whether or not the Speaker can reconcile two of his or her own statements. The Speaker's response, therefore, is not evaluated by the Understander, it is accepted.

In other words, in order to be effective, a challenge must be firmly based in a relationship of trust which in turn features respect, empathy and honesty.

Activities

Activity 9.1

Individual task
☐ Think about the following statements and make a few notes to indicate the extent to which you agree or disagree with them.

a In order to maintain a reasonable atmosphere at work, it is necessary to put up with things from colleagues that one doesn't actually approve of.
b What is essential to a successful language learning group is that the learners feel secure, that they feel the teacher cares about their progress, and that they feel there is some purpose to their work.
c The most common problem faced by teachers has nothing to do with methods, materials or learners: it is their hopelessly low pay.
d We look to Colleges and Faculties of Education to provide trainee teachers not only with theories, but with the fundamental techniques of language teaching: the ability to analyse, present and practise language.

e If someone I work with is unhappy about something I have said or done, I like them to come and tell me about it openly.

f It is unfair to expect teachers to behave as if they are the friends, parents or guardians of their students. One tries to treat students as well as one would treat anyone that one works with, but that is as far as it goes.

Group task

☐ Form a group of three and take it in turns to be the Speaker, the Understander and the Observer.

☐ The first Speaker speaks about **a** and **e**. The second Speaker speaks about **c** and **f**. The third Speaker speaks about **b** and **d**. The Speakers try to put across exactly what they think about each statement.

☐ The Understander supports the Speaker: attending, reflecting and focusing, and listening particularly for opportunities to thematise and to challenge. Remember that the particular purpose of challenging is to ensure that the Speaker's developing ideas are coherent in the Speaker's own terms.

☐ The Observer makes notes on what happens and leads feedback afterwards. Central questions are:

What facial expressions or elements of body language did the Observer notice?

Did the Speaker feel well listened to?

What moves did the Understander make? What language was used?

Particularly, was there any thematising or challenging?

Did the Speaker find the Understander's work helpful?

How did the Understander feel?

Activity 9.2

Individual task

☐ The best teams are made up of members who each bring different strengths. This task invites you to think about your individual contribution to a team. Look at the chart below, which describes team member stereotypes.

Please note that the last column is *not* called *negative qualities*, it is called *allowable weaknesses*. If you have a person with the given strengths in your team, you shouldn't worry too much if they have these weaknesses.

☐ Now, decide which stereotype you think comes closest to describing you. If you find it absolutely impossible to settle for one stereotype, allow yourself a mix of two. But remember, you are not being asked to describe yourself as a stereotype, just to say which one you think comes closest to yourself. The purpose is to use the stereotype as a starting point, not accept it as an endpoint.

Team Roles				
Type	Symbol	Typical features	Positive qualities	Allowable weaknesses
Company person	CP	conservative, dutiful, predictable	organising ability, common sense, hard working, discipline	inflexible, unresponsive to new ideas
Chair	CH	calm, confident, controlled	welcomes all ideas on merit, without prejudice; clear objectives	only ordinary in intellect and creativity
Shaper	SH	highly strung, dynamic, outgoing	lots of drive, challenges inertia and complacency	impatient, easily provoked and irritable
Source	SO	individualist, serious, unorthodox	great intellect, imagination, knowledge	up in the clouds, disregards practical detail and protocol
Investigator	IN	extrovert, enthusiastic, curious	contacts new people, explores new ideas, likes a challenge	loses interest after the initial attraction has passed
Monitor	MO	sober, unemotional, careful	sound judgment, discretion, hard-headedness	lacks inspiration or the ability to motivate others
Team worker	TW	sociable, rather mild, sensitive	responds to people and situations, promotes team spirit	indecisive at moments of crisis
Completer	CO	orderly, painstaking, anxious	follows through to the end, perfectionist	worries about small things, won't 'let go' of a piece of work

Group task

☐ Form a group of three and carry out the following task:

☐ *The Speaker's* aim is to explore the question, *What kind of a team member am I, and how could I be better?* Start from the stereotype that you have chosen as being closest to yourself. Explain in what ways the stereotype describes you and what it misses. Then move in the direction that seems most appropriate in order to explore the above question for yourself.

□ *The Understander's* aim is, of course, to support the Speaker by understanding, using all available skills as appropriate.

□ *The Observer* observes and leads the feedback session. The final notes on the previous activity also apply here.

Activity 9.3

Individual task

□ Answer the following questionnaire for yourself. As with all questionnaires, we want to *use* it, not submit to it. The more truthful you can be with yourself, the more interesting the results will be, but don't agonise over the responses! Respond quickly and honestly and trust your intuitions.

Questionnaire

The beginnings of seven statements are given below. There are eight possible ways to complete each statement (a–h). You have ten points to distribute among the eight responses in an attempt to describe yourself. For each statement, for example, you may give all ten points to one response if you feel that one response describes you exactly. Or you may give one point to each of seven responses and three to the eighth. You can divide the points any way you wish, so long as you give exactly ten points to each statement.

Statements	Points

1 My contribution to a team is that . . .

a I am quick to see new opportunities and take advantage of them. . . . . .
b I can work well with different types of people. . . . . .
c I produce ideas. . . . . .
d I draw people's good ideas out of them. . . . . .
e I make sure that things get done. . . . . .
f I don't mind being unpopular as long as we get results. . . . . .
g I know what is realistic and what will work. . . . . .
h I can put forward a good argument for different ideas. . . . . .

Total points . .10. .

2 A possible weakness of mine in team work is that . . .

a I need meetings to be properly structured and well conducted. . . . . .
b I want everyone to have a chance to express their opinions. . . . . .
c I may talk too much when the group discusses new ideas. . . . . .
d I see the advantages and the disadvantages of ideas, so I don't get too enthusiastic about any one. . . . . .
e I may appear bossy when something needs to be done. . . . . .
f I don't like to lead if that means I'm alone. . . . . .

g I think about my ideas and may lose track of what's
happening.   . . . . .
h I worry about things going wrong and about small details.   . . . . .

Total points   . .10. .

3 When I am working on a project with other people ...

a I can influence people without putting pressure on them.   . . . . .
b I make sure that we don't make careless mistakes.   . . . . .
c I try to keep things moving, so that we don't waste time or
lose sight of our objective.   . . . . .
d I usually contribute something original.   . . . . .
e I am ready to support a good idea from anyone.   . . . . .
f I like to look for new ideas and developments.   . . . . .
g I think my good judgment helps us come to correct
decisions.   . . . . .
h I make sure that all essential work is organised.   . . . . .

Total points   . .10. .

4 My usual approach to group work is that ...

a I have a quiet interest in getting to know people better. . . . . .
b I don't mind challenging people or holding a minority view. . . . . .
c I can usually find a good argument against a bad idea.   . . . . .
d I am good at putting an agreed plan into action.   . . . . .
e I avoid the obvious and come up with something unexpected. . . . . .
f I like to do a job properly once I have started.   . . . . .
g I like to make use of contacts outside the group itself. . . . . .
h I am interested in everyone's views, but I have no trouble in
making a decision when we have to.   . . . . .

Total points   . .10. .

5 I gain satisfaction from a job when I can ...

a analyse situations and consider possible choices.   . . . . .
b find practical solutions to problems.   . . . . .
c encourage good working relationships.   . . . . .
d have a strong influence on decisions.   . . . . .
e meet people who have something new to offer.   . . . . .
f get people to agree on a necessary course of action.   . . . . .
g give my full attention to a task.   . . . . .
h find a field that stretches my imagination.   . . . . .

Total points   . .10. .

6 If I were suddenly given a difficult task with limited time and unfamiliar people ...

a I would like some time to myself in order to decide on the
best way forward.   . . . . .

b I would work with the person who showed the most positive
approach. . . . . .

c I would find out what the people in the team could best
contribute to completing the task. . . . . .

d I would make sure that we did not fall behind schedule. . . . . .

e I believe I would keep cool and think clearly. . . . . .

f I would stick to the job despite the pressures. . . . . .

g I would give a lead if we were not making progress.

h I would start discussions so as to stimulate new ideas and
get things moving. . . . . .

Total points . .10. .

7 As far as my own problems with team work are concerned...

a I get impatient with people who slow the group down. . . . . .

b I am criticised for being too analytical and not intuitive. . . . . .

c I sometimes hold up the proceedings by wanting everything
to be done as correctly as possible. . . . . .

d I may get bored and rely on others to get me going again. . . . . .

e I find it difficult to work unless the goals are clear. . . . . .

f I may have difficulty explaining my complicated ideas. . . . . .

g I know that I demand from others things I can't do myself. . . . . .

h I don't like to argue if someone opposes me. . . . . .

Total points . .10. .

☐ Now transfer your points to the table below.

**Statement
Number**

1	g	d	f	c	a	h	b	e	= 10
2	a	b	e	g	c	d	f	h	= 10
3	h	a	c	d	f	g	e	b	= 10
4	d	h	b	e	g	c	a	f	= 10
5	b	f	d	h	e	a	c	g	= 10
6	f	c	g	a	h	e	b	d	= 10
7	e	g	a	f	d	b	h	c	= 10

☐ Now comes the tricky part. Look back at your scores and add up
the points in their vertical columns. Each vertical column of points
represents one of the stereotype categories that you looked at in
the previous activity, and in the same order that you looked at
them. Your highest score shows which stereotype you come
closest to, according to your responses to the questionnaire.
Your lowest score is the type of which you have the fewest
characteristics. An example looks like this:

Statement
Number

	CP	CH	SH	SO	IN	MO	TW	CO	
1	g.....	d.....	f.....	c..3..	a..3..	h..2..	b.....	e...2.	= 10
2	a..2..	b.....	e..4..	g.....	c..3..	d..1..	f.....	h.....	= 10
3	h.....	a.....	c..5..	d..2..	f..1..	g.....	e..2..	b.....	= 10
4	d.....	h.....	b..5..	e.....	g.....	c..5.	a.....	f.....	= 10
5	b..2..	f..2..	d.....	h..2..	e.....	a..2..	c..2.	g.....	= 10
6	f.....	c..2..	g..4..	a..2..	h.....	e.....	b..2.	d.....	= 10
7	e.....	g..4..	a..4..	f..2..	d.....	b.....	h.....	c.....	= 10
Totals:	4	8	22	11	7	10	6	2	

☐ The questionnaire result may support the comments about yourself that you made in the first place. For some people, however, the type suggested by the questionnaire will be very different from the type they originally chose. Whichever is the case for you, take some time to think about what you have learned, remembering that in both cases the result has come from your own opinions about yourself.

Group task

☐ Ideally, you need to use the same groups that you worked in for activity **9.2**. On this occasion, the same person should be the Speaker and the same person the Understander. The Speaker then carries out the same task. That is, the Speaker's aim is to explore the question, 'What kind of a team member am I, and how could I be better?'

☐ *The Speaker* now has more information to go on than before. Remember, as you explore the second part of the question, none of us can be perfect! If you want to be a better team member, where should you put your efforts, do you think? Into what you're good at, or into what you're bad at?

☐ Once again, *the Understander* aims to support the Speaker. The Understander should try especially to practise thematising and challenging, based on what the Speaker is saying now, and what was said previously.

☐ *The Observer* observes and leads the feedback session. The final notes on Activity **9.1** on page 55 also apply here.

☐ There are more comments on this activity in Chapter 15.

10 Disclosing

All the previous moves available to the Understander have stressed the importance of working in the Speaker's frame of reference. This emphasis remains the same here, which makes *disclosing* a very difficult skill to use effectively.

Let us begin again with a negative description. In normal conversation, we are as free with our experiences as we are with our opinions. So, the following exchange would be quite normal:

> T1: Had a really good class with 4B today.
> T2: Yes, they're a great bunch, aren't they? Did I tell you about that project I did with them last term? It was when . . .

The second teacher takes the first teacher's experience, discloses some common ground with it and takes the conversation off in a direction that will focus on the second teacher's experience. This is normal in conversation, but to be avoided in Cooperative Development.

As an Understander, I will disclose my own experience only to the extent that it may be useful to clarify exactly what the Speaker is trying to say. I may offer an experience of mine in order for the Speaker to use it as a source of comparison or contrast. The frame of reference remains that of the Speaker.

So, there might be an exchange such as this:

> SPEAKER: I always go through homework tasks carefully and check that everyone knows what to do, and we agree that they're going to do it. Then if someone doesn't do it, I find it really difficult to work with that person for a while in the next lesson.
>
> UNDERSTANDER: Mmm. If I've put that much effort in, I feel sort of insulted. Is it like that?
>
> SPEAKER: Oh, no, I wouldn't say insulted. But there's a disappointment that makes things awkward for a while. I have this feeling: 'Why should I bother with you?'

Notice that the Understander is not offering an intellectual opinion, as in a discussion, nor trying to categorise the Speaker's experience. The offering of a personal emotion from the Understander has given the Speaker a point of comparison, and thereby an opportunity to be more exact about what he or she wanted to express. So, here we do have a clear role for the experience and feelings of the Understander, but their use involves a real test of discipline, both for the Understander and for the Speaker. Disclosing must not be used as a covert way of giving advice; it is another technique for aiding clarification of exactly what the Speaker wants to say.

Activities

Activity 10.1

☐ Look back through the previous activities that you have done. See if there is one which you found particularly interesting where you were not the Understander. Carry out that activity again with your colleagues and see if there is an appropriate opportunity to practise disclosing.

Activity 10.2

☐ This task ideally requires a group of at least four people who know each other to some extent and who have established a feeling of reasonable trust. It is a little complicated, so please read all the instructions through carefully, and then follow them one by one. You may want to photocopy the following page and pass that round, rather than use the book itself.

Motivation

Write your name in the space provided and then, in the **Self** column, rank the motivations given by numbering them from 1–10 according to how important they are for you. Number 1 is the most important. Now fold this page so that the **Self** column is hidden from view.

When everyone has finished, put the papers in the centre of the group. Take someone else's paper and rank the motivations according to your view of that person. Do this for other papers until the three **Others** columns are filled for each one.

Take your own form back again, add up the total score that your colleagues have given you for each motivation and enter these in the **Total** column. You can then work out the sequence of motivations that your colleagues have given you (the lowest total is Motivation number 1), and enter this under **Rank**.

You can now compare your opinion of your own motivation with other people's opinion of you.

Name:				**Total**	**Rank**	**Self**
Motivation	**O t h e r s**			**Total**	**Rank**	**Self**
to be liked						
to make a lot of money						
to serve other people						
to have a good time						
to be safe						
to be an expert						
to become well known						
to be independent						
to maximise status						
to be a leader						

☐ Take some time to think about your results.

☐ If you did the above exercise as a group of four, split up now into pairs in order to work as Speaker and Understander. I am suggesting that you do the following activity without an Observer, so that you can see whether you prefer to have one or not. But if it is more convenient to work with an Observer, then you should certainly continue to do so.

☐ *The Speaker's* task is to explore any differences between his or her self-image of motivation and the ranking given by others, in order to discover some grounds for this disparity. The important categories to focus on are those that were ranked 1, 2, 3 or 8, 9, 10 from one perspective or the other. If the scores show that the Speaker's self-image matches the image that other people have of them, an alternative topic for the Speaker to work on would be to talk about how it felt to carry out this task, especially when trying to rank the motivations of others.

☐ *The Understander* supports the Speaker's exploration, using the moves and skills that we have looked at so far, and particularly trying to use the skill of disclosing when this seems appropriate. Remember, the purpose of disclosing is to help the Speaker express more exactly what he or she wants to say by offering a feeling or experience for comparison.

☐ When the Speaker wants to stop, Speaker and Understander should discuss the interaction, with special attention to the use of disclosing and whether or not it was helpful. At this stage you might want to look at the further comments on this activity in Chapter 15.

PART 4
Action

In the same way that teacher development means self-development, Cooperative Development must be Speaker driven. Furthermore, the whole purpose of Cooperative Development is to act. Speakers express their ideas, reactions and feelings about teaching experiences in order to move towards a way of being a teacher that is authentic for each individual. Understanders work to understand (and thus foster) this expression, signalling non-judgmental acceptance, using reflection, focusing, thematising, challenging and disclosing as they seem appropriate.

The final turn towards action opens up more possibilities and responsibilities for Speaker and Understander. These are an involvement in the Speaker's **goal-setting, trialling** and **planning**.

11 Goal-setting

In the drive to develop, it becomes essential for the Speaker to decide on a course of action. For teachers, this course of action will involve some kind of behaviour related to the classroom, followed by the investigation of that behaviour as to its success in moving the Speaker closer to what he or she wants to be doing and achieving.

The spur for this particular action will probably come out of one of three types of realisation. Speakers will realise that:

- they are dissatisfied with what is happening in some area, or
- some particular success deserves wider application, or
- one area of teaching is so interesting as to demand further investigation.

Whatever the motivation, it has to be stressed here that some sort of behaviour is the goal. The time for expression of ideas and values now has to be used in the formulation of a goal that can be specified in terms of action. This is the goal-setting that the Speaker needs to accomplish if Cooperative Development is to move beyond talk.

So, the Speaker referred to above in the chapter on challenging (p.53), might work towards the goal of seriously investigating the use of word-lists for vocabulary teaching in order to see if some learners do respond well to it. Or the Speaker referred to in the chapter on thematising (p.47) might decide to introduce a series of activities which encourage personal investment in order to see if there is any effect on the content of the students' writing. There is no correct goal, or type of goal, except that which provides a next step for the Speaker in the investigation of professional activity.

All the efforts of the Understander are put at the service of the Speaker in this activity of goal-setting. As a particular area of teaching is worked on and a focus found, the aim of the interaction is to decide: *So what? What is to be done?* The overall purpose of the talk is to make sure that what is done is what the Speaker wants to do, based on a coherent foundation of the Speaker's values, experiences and purposes.

Not every session of interaction will necessarily lead to goal-setting in classroom terms. Some sessions will lead to a focus which the Speaker wishes to take away and read about, or a challenge which the Speaker wishes to think more about. These points need to be clarified and worked on. Nevertheless, classroom goal-setting is a recurrent purpose. Furthermore, people who work together on a regular basis, in a regular teaching routine, with regular, mutual class visits, should find that goal-setting becomes an easier and more normal practice.

Cooperating in a regular teaching routine also helps to keep goals to a moderate scale: the smaller the goal, the better the chance of acting towards it and being able to evaluate its worth. Working to such small-scale goals, and getting early feedback, is itself motivating and helps to keep Cooperative Development on the move.

A goal such as, 'I'll find out what the students think about having the reading passage read aloud to them,' is much smaller in scale than the ones used as examples above, but that is its strength. This is a goal which the teacher can aim for in the very next reading class.

So, while goal-setting may begin with a broadly conceived goal, it must then be narrowed down to something that the Speaker can actually undertake as a specific piece of action. This narrowing down process might sound something like this:

SPEAKER: I want to make them see that the novel is relevant to them.

UNDERSTANDER: Have you got any idea of how to go about it?[1]

SPEAKER: Well, I thought of taking the idea of 'jealousy'. That's central to the story.

UNDERSTANDER: Mm–hm.[2]

SPEAKER: I thought I'd get them to talk about jealousy in their own lives, and then get them to see it in the story.

UNDERSTANDER: So the first thing you want to do is to have them discuss their own feelings of jealousy?[3]

SPEAKER: Maybe their own jealousy, but also other people's and the effects it can have.

UNDERSTANDER: Yes. Didn't you say before, 'jealousy in their own lives'?[4]

SPEAKER: Sure. Yes, I did. I mean, it might be their own actual feelings, or it might be what they've seen happen because, say, their sister's boyfriend got jealous, or something like that.

UNDERSTANDER: Got it. So, when they talk about the effects of jealousy, should it be effects they've actually seen or felt, or could it be what they've heard, you know, what everybody says?[5]

SPEAKER: I don't think you can really keep them apart, but I want to get their own experiences involved really, that's the main point.

UNDERSTANDER: OK, so have you got a goal for the next class with them?[6]

SPEAKER: Yes, I think so. I want to set up some sort of discussion activity that will get them talking about their experiences of jealousy in themselves or people they know, and its effects.

UNDERSTANDER: OK, do you want to work on that?[7]

I have numbered the Understander's contributions in the above exchange so that I can more easily make some comments on them. Before I do, you might want to spend a few moments thinking for yourself: 'What was the Understander doing with these different utterances?'

This is what I hear going on:

[1] An open question, encouraging the Speaker to think about implementation.

[2] An extra-linguistic signal of attention, probably accompanied by a nodding of the head or some other sign of encouragement to continue.

[3] Reflecting 'jealousy in their own lives' with 'their own feelings of jealousy'. Notice that the Speaker is not happy with this and says more in order to clarify what was meant.

[4] Challenging the difference between 'jealousy in their own lives' and 'other people's (jealousy)', because the Understander now feels that the Speaker is shifting position without acknowledging the fact, is being unclear and imprecise.

[5] With 'Got it,' the Understander acknowledges the Speaker's sorting out of the challenge, and sees that the Speaker was not being incoherent at all. The Understander then asks the Speaker to set a limit on how general the idea of 'jealousy in their own lives' is meant to be. The use of a closed (either/or) question is not usually as helpful as an open question. Here, a justification might be that the Speaker and the Understander have more or less worked out the two categories of the choice together. In what follows, we see that the Speaker appears to accept the choice the Understander offers and, on this occasion, the Understander's question has helped the Speaker to focus on 'the main point', which is 'to get their own experiences involved'.

[6] The Understander guides the Speaker to the act of goal-setting.

[7] The Speaker has a rough idea of what to do. This is expressed in a series of imprecise expressions: 'some sort of discussion activity'; 'get them talking'; 'experiences of jealousy'; 'themselves or people they know'; 'its effects'. The Understander now signals a desire to help the Speaker to focus further in terms of specific detail.

I hope that the activities which have followed earlier chapters have been interesting for you, have provided good learning opportunities, and have been relevant to your professional development. At this point of your work with this book, I hope that the activities that I invite you to involve yourselves in will become a part of your working life.

Activities

I have reintroduced the Observer in the following activity, but it is entirely your decision as to whether you want to work with an Observer, or to have the Speaker and the Understander deal with feedback discussion themselves.

Activity 11.1

Individual task

☐ Complete the following sentences for yourself. Then see if you can add a sentence or two of your own. Later on, you'll be asked to choose one or two of these sentences to talk about.
  - As a teacher, the type of activity I most enjoy is...
  - As a teacher, the type of activity I least enjoy is...
  - One type of activity I think students learn a lot from is...
  - The kind of change I would like to make in my teaching is...
  - One aspect of my teaching that I'm really pleased about is...
  - One thing I would like to do more of in my teaching is...
  - One thing I don't like about my teaching is...
  - One technique I would like to try out in class is...
  - The kind of student I'm best with is...
  - The sort of student I can't stand is...

Group Task

☐ Sit in a group of three and decide who will be Speaker, Understander and Observer. Carry out the following task.

☐ *The Speaker*: Choose one of the sentences above to talk about. Your aim is to set yourself a goal for a future class. You may start off quite generally, but your purpose is to specify a particular piece of teaching action that you will carry out. If you find it helpful, use the focusing circles approach that we used in Chapter 7. Start by asking yourself, 'What is so interesting about this for me?' and move on to ask, 'What exactly am I going to do about it?'

☐ *The Understander*: Attend carefully. Make the Speaker feel listened to. Use all previously practised skills where appropriate. Listen particularly for any potential focus. The aim is to help the Speaker specify a small scale goal for classroom action.

In goal-setting, it is particularly important that the goal:
- is practical in terms of actual implementation;
- is coherent for the Speaker with his or her stated purposes.

☐ *The Observer*: Pay particular attention to the Understander, noting any non-linguistic communication. Pay special attention to the Understander's attempts to aid goal-setting, noting anything that seems particularly successful or unsuccessful. After not more than fifteen minutes, lead a feedback session, contributing the above information and asking for the reactions and contributions of the Speaker and Understander. The following questions are central:
- Did the Speaker feel 'understood', as we are using the term?
- Did the Speaker find the goal-setting successful and useful?
- How did the Understander feel while trying to aid goal-setting without making his or her own suggestions (i.e. with respect and empathy)?
- How did the Speaker feel when no suggestions were forthcoming?

Activity 11.2

☐ Look back at the following:

Chapter	Activity
7	5
8	1
9	2 and 3
10	2

☐ Working either with or without an Observer, as you prefer, see if you can set yourself a goal on the basis of the work you did or could do in these activities. They will probably not be classroom teaching goals, but you should concentrate on finding a definable action that you can take from which you can learn and develop.

12 Trialling

Once a goal has been set, the work of the Speaker and Understander turns to a detailed, step-by-step blueprint for implementation. The idea is to give the Speaker a chance to talk through what will be necessary before actually having to do it.

In this spoken rehearsal, the Speaker gets a chance to make sure that the steps towards the set goal have been thought through and that they are coherent. The Understander follows the Speaker's description and brings up any points of detail that the Speaker might overlook. These might include, for example, clarification of exact procedure, linking of procedure to purpose, or listing of necessary aids. Thus, both minds combine to diminish the risk of the Speaker's being faced by an unexpected eventuality in class.

At this point, it is important to stress the relationship between careful preparation and flexibility. The purpose of the *trialling* is certainly not to produce a plan that must be followed at all costs. The point here is that the Speaker's course of action towards a goal should be organised and meaningful in its own right. At the same time, let us agree immediately that classrooms are always full of unexpected eventualities and that no amount of preparation can change this. However, when the unexpected happens, it is exactly when one has a systematic plan based on lucid ideas that one is in a strong position to be flexible, to improvise, and to react confidently to the new situation.

Trialling, therefore, is meant to support the development of careful lesson preparation, which can in turn support flexibility and adaptability in a sensitive teacher who is working towards a clear goal.

There is another point to make about the unexpected things that happen in class: they can be very useful learning experiences. So, if I am not able to carry out my plan in one particular class, I don't want to spend my time and energy getting too frustrated about it. I want to learn from the unexpected thing that got in my way. Next time I talk to my Understander, I shall try to focus on this event for a while before I move on to set my new goal for the next lesson, starting from where I am at that time.

In the area of trialling, it can be particularly difficult for the Speaker not to ask for advice or opinions. Again, the fundamentals of this style of cooperation are at issue. As Speaker, I am looking to develop myself to be the best teacher *I* can be. What sounds like a mistake to someone else might not be a mistake for me. If I do plan something that goes wrong, I can live with that and learn from it. The lessons that I learn will also be my own.

It can also be difficult for the Understander not to get involved in making suggestions. As Understander, the underlying principles of respect, empathy and honesty help me to remember that the Speaker is developing as an individual. Certainly, anything that I think I recognise as 'something I have already done' is unlikely to turn out to be a repetition of my experience when someone else does it. The Speaker will learn from it, and so shall I. In fact, those readers who have by now worked as Understander may well be experiencing an extra dimension of growth that I have not previously mentioned: Understanders who do learn to respect and empathise with views other than their own are in a wonderful position to learn new perspectives on old certainties.

To return to our present focus, however, the Understander has to work hard to insist on clarity and detail. During this trialling process, one point about Cooperative Development as a whole should become very clear, if it hasn't already done so! The relationship between Speaker and Understander is not one of wishy-washy warmth and positivity about anything and everything. The Understander wants to accept exactly what the Speaker wants to do, but there is a discipline and a rigour involved in making sure that the Speaker is clear about what that is. The cut-off point is when the Speaker says, 'That's enough. That's how I want to leave it.'

Here is an extended example of two people trialling, having set a goal.

UNDERSTANDER: OK, so if I've got this right, your overall goal is to get the students to pay more attention to the correction that you do of their written work.

SPEAKER: That's right. I think they can learn from it instead of just looking at the mark they get.

UNDERSTANDER: And you said that the only way to do that is to use some class time so that you can make sure that it happens.

SPEAKER: Well, I don't know that it's the only way, but it's the only way I can think of at the moment.

UNDERSTANDER: Right, so . . .

SPEAKER: And it's not just so I can make sure it happens . . .

UNDERSTANDER: Uh-huh . . .

SPEAKER: What I figure is that if I use lesson time, the ones who are interested will see that I really do think that this is important.

UNDERSTANDER: Right you are.

SPEAKER: Let's move on to trialling this and see if I've got it clear.

UNDERSTANDER: OK.

SPEAKER: I'm going to take a piece of their usual written work and just mark one thing in it.

UNDERSTANDER: What's that?

SPEAKER: Well, let's say *a* and *the*.

UNDERSTANDER: Is that an important point for them?

SPEAKER: Yes, it is. They miss the articles out a lot. And we did some revision on them last week.

UNDERSTANDER: OK, but you haven't actually got a piece of work yet to mark?

SPEAKER: No. Let's put it like this. Marking the articles would be a good thing to concentrate on, but if I see something else is obviously more important in that piece of work, I'll go for that.

UNDERSTANDER: Yes, sure.

SPEAKER: Anyway, I'll just underline in the homework any example I see of the particular mistake.

UNDERSTANDER: Nothing else?

SPEAKER: Not this first time, no.

UNDERSTANDER: What if some people haven't got any examples of that mistake?

SPEAKER: Oh, yes. I'll tell you what, then. I'll correct the papers in my usual way, but when it comes to articles, I'll just underline.

UNDERSTANDER: So, they'll still get their usual mark at the bottom.

SPEAKER: That's right. But before I give the papers back, I'm going to put some examples up on the board of where the articles have been missed out or used wrongly. We'll correct them together and talk about why they're wrong.

UNDERSTANDER: How long do you reckon that will take?

SPEAKER: About five minutes.

UNDERSTANDER: Is that enough?

SPEAKER: Well, let's say ten, anyway. Then I'll give out the papers and tell them to work in pairs on correcting their article mistakes.

UNDERSTANDER: Are they OK with pairwork? And for correction?

SPEAKER: I think so. We use pairwork for this and that, and any activity involves some correction. And they mostly sit next to people they like, so I don't foresee any problem there.

UNDERSTANDER: How long?

SPEAKER: Same again, about five to ten minutes. I don't want to spend more than fifteen minutes on this, but I'm prepared for it to take a bit longer this first time, till they get used to the idea.

UNDERSTANDER: What happens then?

SPEAKER: I'm going to collect the papers in again and see what they've done. I can't keep on doing that, it'd be too much work, but I have to make the effort this time, and maybe a couple more times. I have to see if it's working, and show that I think it's worth the effort. Afterwards, I'll maybe just do it now and again. Anyway, I hope that they will see the point and want to do it properly when they see that they can.

UNDERSTANDER: So, the point is to get them better at correcting their own mistakes?

SPEAKER: Yes. If I can establish that, I hope that they can get into doing it without me always having to spend class time on it. And at the same time, I want to find out if getting better at correcting their own mistakes will make them more careful about the mistakes they make in the first place.

UNDERSTANDER: How will you know that?

SPEAKER: I know them!

UNDERSTANDER: Yes, sure, but I mean is there any way of measuring it, though?

SPEAKER: I don't know.

UNDERSTANDER: Do you want to get into working on that?

SPEAKER: Maybe. Let's see how this goes first.

UNDERSTANDER: Yes, yes. Sorry! What are you going to do when you get the papers back?

SPEAKER: Well, I'll check what they've done and make sure that they have a correct script at the end.

UNDERSTANDER: Is that 'correct' altogether?

SPEAKER: No, I mean what they've done about the articles.

UNDERSTANDER: What if they're just a mess?

SPEAKER: I guess I will just have found out that articles were a bad thing to have concentrated on for self-correction, because they haven't got a clue how to use them! But

let's see what we do get back, and then maybe we
could work on that before I decide on what to do
next.

UNDERSTANDER: Great. Do you feel clear about what you're going to do
now?

SPEAKER: Yes, thanks. I'm pleased you made me think about
exactly what marking I would do. That was a help. I
think I can see the whole picture now.

The above dialogue is one that I have reconstructed from a session
that I was once involved in. It gives an example of a Speaker trialling
a teaching procedure with an Understander. It is only one example
towards one particular goal, but I hope that it clarifies what I mean
by trialling.

As I said at the end of the last chapter, I hope that the activities
which you can now base on the techniques of Cooperative
Development will be drawn from your working life, and can
become a part of it.

Activities

Activity 12.1

☐ Take the goal which you set in Activity **11.1**, and trial it with an
Understander, or with an Understander and Observer.

Activity 12.2

☐ Trial any goals that you set from Activity **11.2**.

Activity 12.3

☐ Select another point of interest in your own teaching situation. My
activities have been an attempt to get you into this, but there will
be a better place to start from which only you can know about.
Work from this point with an Understander towards trialling.

13 Planning

This is the final stage of the interaction, where the administrative arrangements for continuity are made. This might, for example, involve fixing details of a class to be watched, and clarifying which aspects of the lesson the Understander should pay particular attention to.

In another instance, the Speaker and the Understander may have come to a point in their interaction at which the Speaker realises a need to find out something more about a topic. The Speaker in the previous chapter (p.72) for instance, might want to find out more about learners' mistakes and ways of correcting them. The *planning* stage, therefore, might involve plans to read something, or consult a particular colleague before the next meeting.

At the very least, it will involve arranging when and where Speaker and Understander will meet again so that the process of Cooperative Development can continue. Cooperation cannot be left to chance. Especially when we are learning a new, disciplined way of working with someone, it is very important that meetings are properly set up and that such agreements are kept to. To make this type of arrangement, of course, Speaker and Understander come out of their roles and plan as two equals in a conversation.

This leads me to two final comments on the relationship between the Speaker and the Understander.

Firstly, this book has concentrated on the development of the Speaker. It is worth repeating, however, that the Understander who learns to help a Speaker develop will hear ideas which might otherwise never have been articulated at all. An Understander can expect to learn a lot through the conventional medium of listening to someone else.

Secondly, there are many other ways in which we learn from each other. There are class visits, ongoing discussions, ideas and materials swapped, and advice given and taken. Nothing that I have said about Cooperative Development is meant to devalue any of these aspects of a teacher's life. Cooperative Development is meant to add to our possibilities by offering a form of interaction which temporarily excludes these aspects of everyday teacher exchange in order to emphasise our abilities to draw upon ourselves. A part of what we have within ourselves to draw on will be made up of the ideas, advice and techniques that we have picked up from colleagues. As we talk these ideas into our own lives, with the help of an Understander, the ideas become our own.

Activities

The activities which you arrange are by now entirely in your own hands. I hope that you will want to arrange regular meetings with colleagues in order to be involved in your own continuing self-development.

The next part of this book sketches the type of context in which Cooperative Development can be useful, and the sources from which it has arisen.

PART 5
Contexts and sources

Chapter 14 looks at contexts in which Cooperative Development can contribute towards the general aim of empowering teachers in their working lives: **teacher development, classroom research, teacher training** and **teacher assessment**.

Chapter 15 goes back over the book, acknowledging where ideas and techniques have come from and suggesting further reading for those who would like to continue their development in this way.

14 Contexts

After using the name Cooperative Development for so long, I think we have earned ourselves an abbreviation, so I shall go on to use what most people who have worked in this area with me call it: CD.

I have said throughout this book that the purpose of CD is *action*. It is perhaps worth expanding that statement here. I do not see the purpose of CD as *change*, because that would be to value change for change's sake. Nor do I see the purpose as *innovation*, because that would be to prejudge the value of the new as compared to the old. Either way, we would be assuming that previous actions were somehow inferior, which is to prejudge both the outcome and the purpose of cooperative interaction.

If a cooperative investigation leads a teacher to feel supported and successful in one area of teaching, then that teacher will continue to act as before, but with an increased sense of confidence and security. This is a perfectly valid outcome of cooperative development.

I am not being altogether straightforward here; I want to involve you in another example of CD. When I expressed the above ideas to a colleague, she said, 'I hear you saying two things, Julian. On the one hand you say that the purpose of CD is not change; on the other hand you talk about a change in attitude being a valid outcome.' And I thought, 'Yes, this is still change. A change in attitude to one's job, and one's confidence in it, is as important a change as a change in behaviour would have been.'

So, my colleague's challenge helped me to develop my thinking in this area. I now say that the purpose of CD is to help us to act in our working lives, and to help us have those actions as close as we can to what we want them to be. The extent to which this will mean that we must change what we do is exactly the question that we are trying to answer. We will answer the question by developing our awareness of our situations, by organising new experiences in those situations, and by trying to express what we have learned.

In very brief terms, I want to look at four areas of our working lives in which CD is relevant: teacher development, classroom research, teacher training, and teacher assessment.

Teacher development

If I say least about this now, I hope that it is nevertheless clear that I consider it to be the most important area of all. I said what I have to say in the opening chapter. Moreover, the whole book is meant to serve the idea that individual teachers can draw on their own experience and intellectual learning and can discover an increasing awareness of what to do by exploring those forms of knowledge with colleagues who have no vested interest in changing them in any way.

Writing this book has had similar significance for me. I have drawn on my twenty years of experiencing and studying ELT, as well as my experience and study of what I am calling CD. I have then expressed what I have to say as clearly as I can to people who I shall never meet. This formulation and expression has, in turn, developed my awareness of the work, and I have written things in the final draft of this book which I certainly did not know when I began it.

We are trained to take writing more seriously than speech. This is probably a good idea, because we can't be there to explain if someone misunderstands us in what we have written. The pity of it is, though, that this 'taking seriously' puts a lot of people off writing about their work at all. When we talk about writing, we start to think about research, and that is a word which puts a lot of people off altogether.

A great pity. Research into classroom learning will be done by teachers, or it won't be done properly at all. We simply have to take control of the word.

Classroom research

I can't think of a better way of telling you what I think about classroom research than to say, 'Classroom research is teacher development made explicit.' In other words, if you are trying to understand what is happening in your classrooms while you are trying to teach, you are involved in teacher development. If you then make a written record of what happened, so that others can read about it, you are involved in classroom research.

I want to extend this idea a little, and I want to do so by stepping outside the format of this book. If you have read this far, you probably also read articles in teachers' magazines and journals. This is where ideas develop before they get into book form. I am going to continue this chapter by including three very short articles that I have written over the last few years. I hope that you will recognise some of the ideas. You may also 'recognise my voice', although my accent will be slightly different from the one you know in this book. All of this is a continuing invitation to you to become involved in compiling the record of what we are doing.

Research and Development

Research in education, like research in second language learning, has failed to deliver very much in return for a lot of effort. I don't think it's too difficult to see why this is so if we start from what we know to be true.

My guess is that most teachers have at some time shared the following experience: You go into a class and teach a certain lesson a certain way; it works brilliantly. You think, 'Smart, I'll do the same with this afternoon's class.' And you do. And it's dreadful, for no apparent reason. Already, this experience raises doubts about the very idea that there is a 'method', good or bad, that can be abstracted from one situation and transported to another, a method into which people can be fitted.

So why have researchers invested so much effort in their controlled experiments and their search for the best method? To a very large extent, because of the historical context we live in. Over the last three hundred years, the word 'science' has come to be associated exclusively with the physical sciences. The methodology of Newtonian physics, with a neutral observer and an external object of investigation, has come to be accepted as the only way to carry out serious study. The purpose of serious study is to break down what we observe into its component parts and then explain the laws of cause and effect governing those parts so that we can better manipulate our environment. The test of serious, scientific research is: Can the results be replicated? If I follow your procedure under the conditions you lay down, can you guarantee that I will produce the same results?

Now, if it's true that most teachers have shared the experience that I recount above, then we all know that we can't even replicate our own results from one class to the next; nor, once we've got a bit of nous, do we expect to any more. We are not engaged in that type of activity. One reason why research has had so little to offer us is that it has been trapped inside a totally unsuitable approach, trapped by historical accident and a desire to prove itself serious and academically respectable. We are in a scientistic cul-de-sac, still aping a form of research that has in many ways been abandoned in the physical sciences in which it was developed.

Action Research, Naturalistic Inquiry, Experiential Enquiry are just some of the terms that have been generated by a growing determination to establish a type of research that will be of use to us in human studies, including teaching. Some features of it seem reasonably clear:

a) learning and teaching have to be investigated as they occur, as fully contextualised, integrated experiences, not controlled experiments;

b) the researcher is not a neutral observer, but a part of the context and will be affected by it;

c) results will not be easily or necessarily generalisable, nor will they be value-free, we must try to make our own values clear;

d) results need not be seen as the outcome of cause and effect, but as the outcome of the reciprocal influence of participants and events;

e) the purpose of individual research is not to produce general laws, but to understand our own situations better and to share that understanding;

f) the purpose of educational research in general is not to produce predictive laws, but to build a body of knowledge that is rich in the lived experience of its practitioners; from this we could all learn.

In other words, our development of ourselves as teachers is the basis of educational research; educational research is teacher development made explicit. If you tell me with all the detail you can muster about your situation, your problem, what you did about it, how it worked out and how things look now, I'm not going to rush off and do what you did, but I am going to think about it and it's going to help me ask better questions about my own situation.

One thing that shouldn't change about research is the responsibility to pay our dues as we go along. I don't think that a newsletter like this should be weighed down with references, but if anybody would like a list, I'd be glad to send them mine – perhaps we could cooperate on making it longer.

Edge (1987).

No proof, no disproof: the search for authenticity

How can we defend the validity of subjective experience as the overriding criterion in our personal research and self-development? I think that there are three strands to this argument and I want to look at them separately before pulling them together.

Firstly, there simply are no objective criteria for the quality of a learning/teaching experience. A teaching idea may work for me and not for you, but that doesn't prove or disprove that the idea was a good one. You can't validate or invalidate my experience any more than I can yours. What we can both do is to try to understand our own experiences and the experiences of others and use that understanding to develop our individual sense of what is authentic for ourselves.

Secondly, the search for objective criteria can lead to people being treated as items in our research projects. I recently heard a speaker on classroom research explain how problematic it is to have to put one's research into the hands of teachers. Ideally, one would want to design 'teacher-proof material' so that the research could be done properly. The same speaker was also very instructive on the occasional need to mislead teachers as to what is being investigated. I don't think that anyone who regards colleagues and students as motivated individuals making their own decisions for their own reasons will find much validity in this approach. Validity is going to be found in a procedure in which we share our purposes and our ideas in a common investigation of our experiences.

Thirdly, a lot of what we know about teaching comes from experience, By that, I don't just mean that as the years go by we pick up more wrinkles. I mean that there is a way of knowing that is different from intellectual knowing or technical knowing, different in nature and acquired differently. To take strong instances from outside teaching, I know what it's like to be threatened at gunpoint; I know what it's like to be called Daddy; supply your own examples. I think we need to be careful here not to get involved in a fashionable pendulum ride on which we abandon intellectual knowledge and technical knowledge altogether, but I also think that establishing the validity of experiential knowledge is at the centre of the struggle to establish the sort of personal research that will enrich our development.

So far, I've suggested that serious research and development in teaching can't be based on an essentially outmoded view of science and that it must:

a) abandon the goal of proof/disproof in favour of the goal of individual authenticity;
b) give due weight to ethical validity in the way that we deal with other people involved in our investigations;
c) give due weight to the experiential knowledge of those involved, as well as to intellectual and technical knowledge.

So, wherever possible, we'll try to cooperate with people. We'll come to an agreement with some language learners and with a colleague or two that we want to investigate, say, the issue of unknown words in a reading text. As soon as an actual question like that is raised, there are so many angles to be covered. What do I tell my students to do when they meet unknown words? How do I help them implement my suggestions? What about my colleagues? What do the students think about our ideas? What do individuals really do in that situation? If what they do and what we suggest aren't mutually supportive, what would be the best way to move? Find better ways to persuade them, or change our suggestions so as to make what they do anyway more effective? Do they become more effective?

We also need to find out about other people's work and to add our own version to the written record that makes experience more widely available. One difficulty will come when we try to share our experiential knowledge. It's hard to articulate such awareness even when you work closely with someone, never mind trying to do it in writing. Some would claim that it is by definition impossible, that what we articulate is always something other than what we know in this sense. Perhaps it is, but the articulation itself is yet another way of learning.

There is no objective end to this process, no proof, no disproof. Validity in research terms and authenticity in terms of personal development seem most likely to be found through collaborative work which enriches and refines subjectivity through inter-subjectivity, and in which outcomes are resolved continuingly for each person by individual acts of evaluation.

Edge (1988).

The least we can do is write to each other

Writing is difficult. What makes writing about our work even harder is that we are faced by very formal constraints on how we are supposed to present our ideas. So, very few people write. And some that do write are turned down because their writing doesn't meet the formal requirements.

This is a losing situation. Let's start somewhere else.

Courtesy of the British Council, I have just (December 1989) spent two weeks in India, working with teachers of English, teacher trainers and lecturers in associated fields. (And let me take this chance to thank them again for their hospitality and enthusiasm.)

In one place, I was present at the formation of a new teachers' group aiming at cooperation and professional development. In another place, I listened to a teacher argue for the extension of the responsibility of teachers' groups to include localised materials production in place of set textbooks. In yet another, I heard a man in charge of an institution that runs courses for teachers affirm that the best way forward in the Indian situation was to make audiotapes of ideal lessons. Then the teachers would only have to play these tapes and supervise the learners.

At Lucknow airport, there is a plaque on the wall with quotations from Pandit Jawaharlal Nehru. One of them goes roughly something like this: 'India will be what we are. If we are big and courageous in our thoughts and actions, India will be big and courageous. If we are small and narrow minded, so will India be.'

Much of the work I was doing concerned developing an ability to listen carefully to someone else and to reflect that person's position from their point of view. My worst moment came with one question over tea: 'It's easy for me to reflect his ideas, because he's my boss. But how can he reflect mine?'

A great moment was when a participant said, 'I knew I had some problems, but now I find I have some answers as well.'

Imagine a planet where the richest and most powerful countries develop a tradition of teaching classes of a hundred students. The best educational minds of each generation apply themselves to perfecting the best language teaching methods. One year, another planet is discovered: a poor, sparsely populated planet where life is hard and learners meet only in groups of ten.

Imagine the problems of applying good methods in these impoverished circumstances. How can one adapt the ideal ten groups-of-ten communing technique to a context where one has only ten individuals to work with? Every day, teachers all over this poor planet trudge to work with this and similar problems to contend with.

This is an unfair analogy. And sometimes I exaggerate. But why *should* we believe that the way ahead lies only in the application and adaptation of other people's solutions? Of course we can learn from other people, but we can best *act* out of an understanding of our own situation.

I don't have any understanding of the Indian situation. As I've already said, I've listened to very different understandings of the Indian situation. My guess is that there are as many different Indian situations as there are people thinking about it.

When I lived in Jordan, I heard a story about an old man who had two sons. One day, the elder son wanted to go to Damascus. The old man gave him money and his blessing. When he returned, the son said that Damascus was an awful place, full of violence, cheats, thieves and whores. 'My son,' said the old man, 'I believe you, and I am happy that you have returned to us.'

Sometime later, the second son wanted to go to Damascus. The old man gave him money and his blessing. When he returned, the son said, 'Father, Damascus is a wonderful place, full of music and art, learned discussion and endless libraries.' 'My son,' said the old man, 'I believe you, and I am happy that you have returned to us.'

We have to get beyond our isolated, individual experiences. Our way forward as teachers must surely be to meet and talk about our teaching, and then to trust each other enough to visit each other's classes. And then to talk and plan some more.

But there does need to be more. We are *language* teachers, for goodness' sake. Wouldn't it be irresponsible to deny the importance of written communication, or to give it up because of other people's rules of expression? In the broadest sense, we have to talk to each other. That talk has to include writing to each other. We have to keep a record. We have to keep in touch.

An idea that attracts me is a circular newsletter among teachers or teachers' groups. A teacher in one group has an idea for a lesson that he or she tries out. The teacher then writes up what happens in some kind of class report plus comments. This page or two gets passed to another teacher who tries out the idea and adds a few paragraphs of comments and suggestions based on experience. This document gets added to and passed on among teachers and/or teachers' groups.

After an agreed time or number of teachers, the report is returned to the original teacher. This person, or perhaps a colleague, undertakes to photocopy the whole document and circulate it to contributors, or to put together a synopsis for circulation.

I think that such newsletters, working on a small scale, could contribute to the building of a fund of local knowledge. It might help bring together the knowledge we gain from reading and listening, the knowledge we gain from experience, and the knowledge we gain from trying to express ourselves to others.

On the basis of local knowledge, we might look for the development of local theory. I mean theory in the sense of an informed insider's understanding of our own situation as we live it, not as what others might wish to categorise as a set of problems according to comparison with their situation.

A very sympathetic woman with a PhD in mathematical modelling told me that this is a highly idiosyncratic use of the term *theory*, but I can live with that as long as I find the concept defensible.

Local theory means local understanding of local data: the shared ways that insiders have of making sense of their experiences. Each person's experience and understanding can, if articulated, serve to illuminate the experience and understanding of another, without claiming to explain, predict or evaluate that other. As common ground and respected difference is built in one situation, the illumination of other situations becomes possible.

I understand teacher development and teachers' groups to be about our empowerment of ourselves as teachers, beyond the training courses that are arranged for us.

The idea is relatively new in ELT, and we are still developing the lines and styles of communication that will help this empowerment. I feel that we really must come to command our own lines of written communication as well as spoken.

We can learn to express ourselves in approved ways. We can also work to loosen up what is formally approved by demonstrating that we have things to say in our own ways. We can work to establish our own lines of communication and our own styles.

But one way or another, the least we can do is write to each other. It has become a part of the job.

Note

Much of this arose out of a conversation with Robert Bellarmine. Thanks.

Edge (1990).

Classroom research needs the clearly expressed experiences and ideas of aware insiders – of teachers committed to their own development. Cooperative Development aims to provide a way to help teachers work together in a way which encourages them to formulate their own views of their own actions. If more teachers would keep and share reports of their experiences and observations, we could begin to build up the kind of knowledge base that would make educational research much more meaningful than it has been so far.

Teacher training

If, in the future, teachers are to cooperate with each other in a more meaningful way than they have to date, then this ability to cooperate will have to be learned. In this sense, a scheme such as CD should have a place in any pre-service teacher training course.

On in-service courses, where time is usually shorter, CD can be introduced as the central purpose of a short course, with the content of the introductory activities drawn from the teachers' own situations. In this way, the course might hope to have a lasting influence on the teachers' work, as it introduces a method of continuing autonomous development.

Once teachers are familiar with CD, it provides an appropriate central method for running in-service courses. Participants on such courses frequently complain that trainers either don't know enough about the teaching situation, or don't pay enough attention to its constraints. CD procedures encourage participants to work with each other from a position of inside knowledge. When they have set goals, they will listen with interest to ideas and suggestions from others in a more usual, ideas-exchanging or discussion format. Participants will then evaluate what they have heard from trainers and from peers, and will articulate their own positions as they try to tighten up their goals and trial their own responses.

So far, I have been talking about how CD might be introduced for teachers to use among themselves. There is a different question regarding CD in teacher training: can trainers and trainees participate together in CD? There is no clear cut answer of the yes/no variety, but we can make some general comments.

It is often the case that people who have learned to listen and respond in the kind of way that CD offers become more open to the idea that other people have valid viewpoints which differ from their own. They also become more sensitive to the needs of other people to have their say. To this extent, CD can be useful to trainers in the effect that it has on them in their work with trainees. Conversely, as it builds up the confidence of trainees in their ability to develop their own position, the effect of CD experience can be useful to trainees in their work with trainers. Also, experience as Understander can help aware trainees recognise the frequent need of trainers to be taken seriously as teachers.

Ultimately, however, we are talking here about the effect of CD experience rather than an ongoing CD relationship. As far as CD itself is concerned, the question about the trainer/trainee relationship comes down to this: to what extent do trainers see it as their responsibility to change the views and behaviour of trainees? To what extent do trainees see it as the trainers' responsibility to tell or show them what to do and how to do it? As long as one participant is seen as taking on responsibility for the views and actions of the other, Cooperative Development is not a real possibility. There would always be a lingering question mark about the honesty of the interaction and the likelihood of manipulation by the (trainer) Understanders towards their own overriding aims. From the other perspective, the (trainee) Speakers might infer guidance where (trainer) Understanders had not meant to give any.

Cooperative Development is meant for use between peers (whether teachers or trainers), where status is not an issue. Some trainers and trainees will be able to use it in some of their work with each other, but it will not be the norm. Having said that about teacher training, what can one say about teacher assessment?

Teacher assessment

Where teacher assessment is seen as a matter of superiors giving marks to inferiors, Cooperative Development can have little part to play. In the long term, we can hope that cooperation and classroom research by teachers might begin to produce more meaningful categories of assessment than we often see on the checklists that are used by inspectors and examiners.

In the short term, however, there are other uses for a CD approach. Some institutions and employers do see that teachers who are encouraged to become involved in assessing their own work are likely to increase their commitment to the job. In this sense, teachers who are regularly setting their own goals and evaluating the results that they achieve as they work towards them are already involved in a form of self-assessment.

This process can be adapted to form the basis of a formal assessment procedure in which teachers take the role of Speaker in order to clarify with management what their goals are for a future period, and how they fared in the implementation of goals set previously. Such a procedure would, clearly, place a great pressure on the honesty of the Understander for as long as the management representative was acting in that role.

Conclusion

In this chapter, I have looked at different professional contexts in which CD might have a role. Let me end by stressing once more the central idea that the Speaker and the Understander, for as long as they are in those roles, must be functioning as equals, with all that that means in terms of respect, empathy and honesty.

15 Sources

In this final chapter, I intend to go back over the contents of the book and refer wherever possible to the people and publications that I have drawn on. There are many more books and articles available in each area than anyone could ever read but, in this way, I can acknowledge my own debts and, at the same time, point a possible way forward to readers who want to follow up any particular area. All the publications I refer to are listed fully in the *References* section after this chapter. My sincere apologies to anyone whose work I have inadvertently failed to acknowledge properly.

Chapter 1   Individuals and colleagues

Self-development and cooperation are the themes underpinning the Teacher Development Special Interest Group of the International Association of Teachers of English as a Foreign Language. There is a newsletter, *Teacher Development*, through which members share their ideas and experiences. My two short articles, 'Research and Development' and 'No proof, no disproof', reproduced in Chapter 14, are taken from the newsletter. If you are interested in joining, the address to write to is IATEFL, 3 Kingsdown Chambers, Kingsdown Park, Tankerton, Whitstable, Kent, CT5 2DJ, England.

The importance of trying to understand human activities from the insider's perspective, and not just as they are observed by outsiders, is being more and more acknowledged. There is, however, still a long way to go. Freire (1972) deals with the sociopolitical and educational aspects of this issue and Geertz (1983) builds an ethnographic view. Ochsner (1979) has written an interesting paper on second language acquisition from this perspective, and issues arising are further expanded in Guiora (1983). References given below for Chapters 2 and 14 are also relevant here.

In its commitment to a belief in the strength of the aware individual, teacher development has much in common with an attitude to teaching that is often referred to as *humanistic*. Underhill (1989) brings out these connections in a very thoughtful way and

Stevick (1990) provides further background. There is also a strong connection with teaching that is sometimes called *learner centred* (Brandes and Ginnis 1986).

Chapter 2   Learning and knowing

There is a long history of philosophical discussion in this area. In using the terms, *experiential understanding, intellectual comprehension,* and *expression*, I am drawing explicitly on the nineteenth century German philosopher, Dilthey (Dilthey 1976). His terms were: *Erleben, Verstehen, Ausdrücken.*

It is the last of the three that receives most attention here. I am looking for a term which captures the idea of a person giving their own shape to the mixture of experience and comprehension that makes up an individual. Perhaps *formulate* would be a better term, but this might be understood as purely mental, and the argument is that, give or take personal styles, the act of communication helps develop formulation. *Articulate* seemed another likely candidate for naming this way of learning, but it seems to lack the affective resonance which is an important part of *expression*. Perhaps this is too much agonising over terminology, but the names that we give exercise a powerful influence on how we understand. If this last point interests you, it can be followed up educationally in Freire (1972) and linguistically in Lakoff and Johnson (1980).

Chapter 3   A way of interacting

The rules according to which we interact linguistically with each other under normal social circumstances make up a fascinating study in their own right. Coulthard (1985) is a good introduction.

The ideas on *respect, empathy* and *honesty* are taken directly from the work of Carl Rogers (1983). It would be difficult to overemphasise the importance of Roger's work to what I am trying to do here. Given his massive contribution, I am picking away at one application. The terms, again, are open to debate. Perhaps *acceptance* would be more directly descriptive than *respect*, but *respect* seems the more person oriented and fundamental term: one accepts because of respect. *Genuineness* might be preferable to *honesty*. I prefer the latter because it confronts directly the frequent question, 'Am I being honest if I don't tell someone I disagree with them?'

The interactive moves which I list and then use to organise the rest of the book are my selection and adaptation from the work of Richard Egan (1986). I was first introduced to this model by Ruby Caldicott at the University of Durham, and the impression that this introduction made on me was the basis of my motivation to work in this way. The influence also shows in some of the activities. Heron (1986) provides another approach to formalised interaction.

Having acknowledged Rogers and Egan, I want to make a point which I consider essential to my own work, to what I am calling Cooperative Development. I very deliberately do not use the term *counselling*, and this decision/omission needs to be commented on. Cooperative Development is not counselling in either of the two ways the term is usually understood.

Firstly, Cooperative Development is not *counselling* in the social or clinical sense of the term. There is no sense in which teachers involved in Cooperative Development should be categorised as 'having problems'; they are committed to developing according to their own purposes.

Nor should Cooperative Development mean becoming involved in the personal problems or traumas of a colleague. That is to say, teachers should not take on such responsibilities any more than they would otherwise do in their relationship with a colleague. Most importantly, the techniques we have learned here should not be misused in areas for which we are not qualified. In Cooperative Development, there is no *counsellor/client* relationship. People who believe in the desirability of counselling as a form of therapy or personal development should inform themselves of where properly qualified counsellors are available. If friends or colleagues are interested in or in need of such services, they can then be put in touch with qualified people. For those who want to read more about counselling, a very accessible introduction to the field is Nelson-Jones (1983).

It is precisely because the word *counselling* carries with it for many people the psychological associations of therapy and trauma that I avoid using it. I realise that I may be accused of thus perpetuating an over crude understanding of the term, but I find that preferable to confusing a useful mode of cooperation between teachers with a form of psychotherapeutic treatment in which the unqualified should not dabble.

Secondly, Cooperative Development is not *counselling* in the sense that this term is most often met in the educational literature (e.g. Stones 1984, Handal and Lauvas 1987). This use of the term regularly refers to a style of teacher supervision which is based on some variant of a trainer/trainee relationship. I have absolutely no wish to attack either this usage, or the style of work involved, which I believe is responsible for much of the best work currently being done in teacher training/education. Once again, however, the fundamental relationship is not the one we are working with in Cooperative Development. I return to this area below in relation to Chapter 14.

Chapter 4 Notes on the activities

The teachers I refer to are Khanum, Malik and Syed (1990), whose work in Cooperative Development was not only very rewarding in its own right, but also encouraged me to believe that I was not indulging myself in a strictly culture-bound form of activity.

Background culture and social norms will, of course, have a continuing effect on what is and is not possible for people. However, having spent twenty years working in ELT in many countries and with multinational groups of teachers in Britain, I find it easy to celebrate our cultural diversity while celebrating our common humanity, while celebrating our individual differences. I am very happy for individuals in their cultures to decide whether or not Cooperative Development can be useful to them. I find it less easy to empathise with people who want to make facile generalisations about what is or is not appropriate to particular cultural backgrounds. I comment on this theme further in the short article, 'The least we can do is write to each other', which is reproduced in Chapter 14.

Chapter 5 Attending

Activity 5.1: A lot of people react negatively to stereotypical comments such as these. Let me tell you about one of my own reactions. I read that to sit with one's legs crossed as below (from Pease 1981) is a sign of potential aggression.

'This is obvious nonsense,' I thought. 'I always sit like that. I can't cross my legs any other way and be comfortable.' This is true. But I then have to ask myself why it is that I have grown to be comfortable with my legs crossed in this way. One explanation is that there is a lot of aggression in my personality. I am still thinking about it.

Pease (1981) is easy to read, clearly illustrated and often amusing. One should note, however, that the book was written essentially for the purposes of doing business and selling things. In other words, the information is presented as a tool for effective manipulation. This is a long way from my purposes in studying the area. A more academic approach to the topic in general is Knapp (1978).

Activity 5.2: Pease's commentaries on the illustrations are as follows:

5.2.a The man on the left is using an excellent gesture cluster to convey openness and honesty – exposed palms, foot forward, head up, coat unbuttoned, arms and legs apart, leaning forward and smiling gestures. Unfortunately for him, however, his story is not going across. The woman is sitting back in her chair with her legs crossed away (defensive), she has a partial arm-barrier (defensive), a clenched fist (hostile), head down and is using the critical evaluation gesture (hand to face). The man in the middle is using the raised steeple gesture, indicating that he feels confident or superior, and he is sitting in the figure 4 leg position, showing that his attitude is competitive or argumentative. We assume that his overall attitude is negative, as he is sitting back, his head down.

5.2.b The man on the left is straddling his chair in an attempt to take control of the discussion or to dominate the man on the right. He is also using the direct body point at the man on the right. He has clenched fingers and his feet are locked together under his chair, showing a frustrated attitude, which means that he is probably having difficulty in getting his point across. The man in the centre feels superior to the other two because of the hands-behind-head gesture he has taken. He also has the figure 4 leg lock position, meaning that he will compete or be argumentative. He has a high-status chair that swivels, leans back and has wheels and arm rests. The man on the right is seated on a low-status chair that has fixed legs and no accessories. His arms and legs are tightly crossed (defensive) and his head is down (hostile), indicating that he does not buy what he hears.

5.2.c In this scene the man on the left and the woman have mirrored each other's gestures and are forming 'bookends' on the couch. The couple are very interested in each other and have positioned their hands in such a way that they can expose their wrists and they have crossed their legs toward one another. The man in the middle has a tight-lipped smile which can make him appear interested in what the other man has to say but it is not consistent with his other facial and body gestures. His head is down (disapproval) his eyebrows are also down (anger) and he is giving the other man a sideways glance. In addition to this, his arms and legs are tightly crossed (defensive), all indicating that he has a very negative attitude.

Activity 5.6: As a prelude to this activity, **A** and **B** can sit opposite each other for two minutes simply looking at each other's faces. Whether or not one begins in this way, this is an activity which involves time, patience and silence – all highly rare and valuable commodities. For some people, it can be highly illuminating to take on the expressions and posture of someone else, and to follow the tiny movements that they make. It can also help to build a feeling of empathy.

I don't feel that it is a good idea to guess or discuss what **A** was thinking about, but this will depend on the people concerned. The deeper **A**'s involvement, the greater the potential of the exercise, but the less the participants might want to talk about it in detail. In such cases, a simple comment such as, 'Sad' or 'Excited' can be all that is needed.

I have adapted this activity from one which I experienced at an introductory workshop in Neurolinguistic Programming run by Tom Willingson. The aspect of NLP highlighted here is the intimate linkage between posture, expression and thought, also the possibility for some people that they will increase their feeling of empathy if they mirror the position and movements of their partner. Once again, we are in an area where we are looking for insights into ourselves as Understanders, and must take care that we do not use such information manipulatively. The basic reference for Neurolinguistic Programming is Bandler and Grinder (1979), and a short education-related article is Arnold and Swaby (1984). If you become interested, look out for an introductory workshop.

Chapter 6 Reflecting

Activity 6.4: I have adapted this activity from Weeks, Pedersen and Brislin (undated), which contains many useful exercises for cross-cultural awareness raising. I have found this particular activity very rich in its outcomes, and very good at building up a desire in Understanders to make their own positions clear! I recognise that some people find difficulty in getting involved in this type of activity; it is too 'artificial' for them. My feeling is that if one can accept activities as vehicles for experience, an authentic experience can validate the use of an activity, no matter how artificial it might initially appear in itself.

Chapter 7 Focusing

The technique of using what I have called *Focusing circles*, comes from Brandes and Ginnis (1986). As I have already said, this book highlights the connections between the interests of the autonomous teacher and the autonomous learner.

Activity 7.5: I have adapted the questionnaire from Plant (1987). One of our weaknesses in education is that we often lag behind work that is being done in the world of commerce, where the need to encourage people to fulfil their aspirations is often recognised as one of the keys to overall success. One of our weaknesses in ELT is that we are often woefully ignorant of what is known in the field of general education.

Chapter 8 Thematising

Activity 8.1: I have taken the first part of this activity from John Morgan who I saw use it in 1987. There is another issue to ponder here, if you wish to. Do you believe that some human activities are in themselves of higher quality than others, rather like the way in which different dives in a diving competition have a difficulty rating? Alternatively, if you work on appreciating yourself and your qualities, can you get as much satisfaction out of, say, washing the dishes as you can out of climbing a mountain, or playing a piece of music (supply your own examples)? Whether you believe that different experiences have a different 'quality count', or whether you believe that there is really only a 'quality of self', there will be an outcome for you in terms of what quality of experience you believe you can get from your teaching. This question arose for me out of a conversation with Adrian Underhill, and I hear echoes of his voice in my use of *outcomes* in the previous sentence.

Activity 8.2: The individual task, using the pattern, or *mandala*, is taken from Zdenek (1985). Zdenek's book has a collection of exercises which are intended to stimulate the functioning of the right hemisphere of the brain, and thus our holistic perceptions, as opposed to the usually dominant analytical processing of the left hemisphere.

Even after this one brief exercise, I have found that an interesting number of people find differences between the two lists of adjectives that they produce. While the first list tends towards the critical and/ or the intellectual, the second list tends towards the more affective aspects of a person's character, often emphasising their vulnerability. I have no wish to exaggerate the effect of what is happening here, I can only report that I have found the exercise interesting enough, often enough, to want to include it. As I said in Chapter 4 about all these exercises, their main function is not to come up with answers or categorisations, but to encourage people to start to talk about themselves.

Zdenek's claim is that her programme of exercises helps to

stimulate non-linear, creative thinking. This is something to be followed up if you find the idea attractive. There is also an extensive literature on neurolinguistics in second language acquisition, which is reviewed in Genesee (1988). Scovel (1982) also writes on this topic and dismisses attempts to relate such work to classroom teaching. My own feeling is that we should inform ourselves of what is going on and where possible try out in class things that seem intuitively interesting. That way, we get involved in the kind of research that only teachers can do, and we can inform the experts of what is interesting to us and what they might usefully continue to investigate in their own contexts.

Chapter 9   Challenging

Activity 9.2: I have adapted the questionnaire slightly from Everard and Morris (1985), who in turn took it from Belbin (1981). Once again, let me stress that the importance of the categories and the questionnaire is to give some initial structure to our own thoughts about ourselves. I hope that it is clear that it would defeat the object of the work if we were to end up trying to fit people into categories.

I'd like to add a personal note here. Like many people, the category I initially put myself in was not the one that I produced by answering the questionnaire. Again like many people, I responded to the result of the questionnaire by looking immediately at the 'allowable weaknesses' and reacting to them as if they were 'negative characteristics'. 'Ridiculous!' I snorted to myself. 'Impatient? Easily provoked!? Who's easily provoked? I'm not easily provoked!' I learned a lot from this questionnaire. By turning it into an interactive exercise, I am hoping that you will learn even more.

Chapter 10   Disclosing

Activity 10.2: This question of image and self-image is very important in our interaction with others. Let's assume for example, that I see my major motivation as a desire to *serve other people*. Several of my colleagues, however, think that I am mostly motivated by a desire to *maximise status*. One day, there is a request for someone to organise an open day for prospective students. When I volunteer for this task, it is with the thought, 'I can do this work, save everyone else the bother, and provide a useful service.' But my colleagues are thinking, 'There goes Julian again, trying to be in charge of everything.'

This clash between my self-image and the image that others have of me means that my actions will have meanings different to those I intend them to have. And anything that I do to try to make things better is just as likely to make things worse, unless I realise the kind of image that other people do have of me.

As in the last chapter, the questionnaire base of this activity is taken from Everard and Morris (1985). Anyone who wants to follow up the social or psychological side of motivation should read their Chapter 3. This includes a brief summary of Maslow's (1943) classic work on motivation. The best known feature of Maslow's work is probably his *Hierarchy of Needs*, which suggests that the type of motivation that we feel will depend on our having satisfied our needs at a lower level of the hierarchy. Thus if I am in extreme physical danger I shall be highly motivated to escape from that danger; I shall not worry about whether my behaviour is likely to win me the respect of society at large.

Maslow's Hierarchy of Needs

SELF-REALISATION
Psychological growth
Achievement

EGO
Status
Respect
Prestige

SOCIAL
Friendship
Group acceptance
Love

SECURITY
Freedom from danger
Freedom from want

PHYSIOLOGICAL
Food, drink, shelter, sex,
warmth, physical comfort

This hierarchy raises issues beyond those which I can go into here. There are three points, however, which I always keep in mind.

The first is an observed tendency in human beings to set their own motivations higher up the hierarchy than they set other people's. So, while I might see myself as trying to write this book in a search for self-fulfilment, I can't avoid the suspicion that a certain person well known to us all wrote his last book just to show off. I neither like nor trust thoughts like this. Until I can get rid of them, I am at least trying to be more aware of them.

The second thought is particularly relevant to people who work with others who are facing a much more difficult social and economic situation than they are themselves. I think of my work with some teachers in Egypt and Turkey, where my monthly salary looked more like their income for a year. The point is that I assumed a kind of motivation that took very little account indeed of their need to hold down two or three jobs in order to house, feed and clothe their families. It is a tribute to them, and humbling to me, to think how many of them made greater efforts than I knew properly how to appreciate.

This brings me to the third point: that some people find motivation at a higher level of the hierarchy which enables them to put up with dissatisfaction lower down. In other words, it is more important for some people to pursue their aspirations than to solve their problems. This is an important point to work on for people with managerial responsibilities.

Chapter 14   Contexts

Here, we really do run into a huge background literature, of which I can only offer the references that I have found especially useful.

Teacher Development

I have given my central references already: the IATEFL TD Newsletter, Rogers (1983) and Underhill (1989) would be good places to start. Before I move on to the other areas, however, I'd like to make a few personal acknowledgements with regard to my own development.

Louis Sassi taught me Latin at school in the 1960s, and intuitively knew more about how to teach a language as though it mattered among people than any teacher of a living language that I have ever had. Caring as much about learners as he did, Sassi then retrained as a counsellor. After a few years in his new role, cuts in educational funding and redefinition of educational policy meant that school counselling posts were discontinued and he retired early. An unforgivable waste. Salve, Louis!

Stevick (1980) was a book which had a big influence on my development as a teacher, not because of the details of the teaching methods described in it, but because the whole book is so resonant of a healthy relationship between shared humanity and individual diversity. That is what I take the subtitle, *A Way and Ways*, to refer to.

In 1982, I was a participant in a workshop run by Mario Rinvolucri, and many of the ideas that I had comprehended in books such as Stevick, above, I now understood. Once again, it was not the detail of method or technique that was most important, but the opening up of a new part of myself for investigation and investment in teaching. Rinvolucri has not written much *about* ELT (but see Rinvolucri 1981), but has written a great deal *for* it; Morgan and Rinvolucri (1986) and Davis and Rinvolucri (1990) are good examples.

As far as CD itself is concerned, I sincerely want to thank the teachers that I have worked with in many places. Apart from the ones I have already mentioned, Shazreh Hussain, Bill Johnston, Cathie Lacey and Stuart Marriott were especially helpful in commenting on earlier drafts of this book. Lacey (1990) is a further source of insight.

Classroom research

The teacher-as-researcher is a well known concept in the field of general education. Hopkins (1985) for the practice and Ruddock and Hopkins (1985) for the background are good places to start reading. Perhaps the reason that the idea still sounds so strange in the ELT world is because it is still convenient for many to continue the fiction that ELT is a sub-branch of linguistics. In this dominant framework, 'research' means doing linguistic research along lines to be stipulated by linguists. 'Classroom research', therefore, can be interpreted to mean the activity of researchers from various allied disciplines taking the classroom and its denizens as the objects of their study.

This picture is slowly changing, however, and one can see new outlines of possibilities for the autonomous teacher/researcher being sketched in Wright (1987), Clark (1987), van Lier (1988), Nunan (1989a) Wallace (1991) and Allright and Bailey (1991). What motivates me is the investigation of my own classrooms as an insider, whether I am teaching English to beginners or discourse analysis to MA participants. I hope it is clear why I see teacher development and classroom research as two sides of the same coin. The role of CD in this context is to enable colleagues to collaborate as effectively as possible in the pursuit of the understanding of their own classrooms; that is, in meaningful educational research.

Anyone who finds this prospect attractive might be interested in joining the IATEFL Research SIG. You can write to the same address as given for the TD SIG in the notes on Chapter 1. Another relevant address is: Classroom Action Research Network, School of Education, University of East Anglia, Norwich NR4 7TJ.

To pursue the more theoretical end of how research into human beings can escape from the confines of 'scientific' ways of investigation, the discussion in Guba and Lincoln (1982) is excellent, and major sourcebooks of discussion and case study are Reason and Rowan (1981) and Reason (1987). Directly related to ELT is Brumfit's (1984: Chapter 1) discussion and the papers collected in Guiora (1983).

Teacher training

I have already pointed out (notes on Chapter 3, above) that there is a possible confusion between CD and what is often referred to as a 'counselling approach' in teacher training. In the final analysis, it is for each individual to decide on the compatibility of an essentially asymmetrical power relationship with the fundamental issues of *respect, empathy* and *honesty.*

Apart from Stones (1984) and Handal and Lauvas (1987) already mentioned, very useful in the area are Freeman's (1982 and 1989) articles, Nunan (1989b) and Wallace (1991).

Once again, there is an IATEFL SIG for teacher trainers, the address for which is given in the notes on Chapter 1, above.

Teacher assessment

Baker (1984) presents a collection of papers on self-evaluation of teachers generally, while Moyles (1988) focuses on the primary teacher in general education. Williams (1989) details an observation based scheme for ELT which could certainly be adapted to contextualise CD in at least some of its parts.

We are in all probability a long way away from a time when teacher self-assessment will be the norm in any form of education. It is also the case that a great number of well intentioned teachers at all levels find the very idea of assessment distasteful. But to the extent that we can make assessment mean *the giving of feedback necessary to further development,* it has to be as much a part of our empowerment as any other aspect of teacher development. And in the taking on of that responsibility, I am sure that our exploration and discovery can prepare us to act towards making assessment more meaningful than it is today.

In conclusion

Teacher development represents a dual purpose for me. Firstly, my own continuing development remains a strong motivation. Secondly, the facilitation of teacher development has become that part of my work which gives me most satisfaction.

Just as teacher development is my purpose, CD has become my way towards that purpose in both its aspects. My primary intention in writing this book is to offer CD as a way which some colleagues will find useful as they clarify and act towards their own purposes.

There will doubtless be other outcomes for readers and participants to discover and evaluate for themselves.

References

ALLRIGHT, R and BAILEY, K M 1991 *Focus on the Language Classroom* Cambridge University Press

ARNOLD, D E and SWABY, B 1984 'Neurolinguistic applications for the remediation of reading problems' *The Reading Teacher* 37.9: 831–834

BAKER, P (ed.) 1984 *Practical Self-Evaluation of Teachers* Longman/Schools Council

BANDLER, R and GRINDER, J 1979 *Frogs into Princes: Neurolinguistic Programming* Real People Press, Moab, Utah

BELBIN, M 1981 *Management Teams: Why They Succeed or Fail* Heinemann

BRANDES, D and GINNIS, P 1986 *A Guide to Student-Centred Learning* Blackwell

BURGESS, R 1985 *Field Methods in the Study of Education* The Falmer Press

BRUMFIT, C J 1984 *Communicative Methodology in Language Teaching* Cambridge University Press

CARR, W and KEMMIS, S 1986 *Becoming Critical: Knowing Through Action Research* The Falmer Press

CLARK, J L 1987 *Curriculum Renewal in School Foreign Language Learning* Oxford University Press

COULTHARD, R M 1985 *Introduction to Discourse Analysis* Longman

DAVIS, P and RINVOLUCRI, M 1990 *The Confidence Book* Longman

DILTHEY, W 1976 *Selected Writings* edited and translated by H P Rickman Cambridge University Press

EDGE, J 1987 'Research and Development' *Teacher Development* 7: 11 (IATEFL)

EDGE, J 1988 'No proof, no disproof: the search for authenticity' *Teacher Development* 8: 2–3 (IATEFL)

EDGE, J 1990 'The least we can do is write to each other' *Focus on English* 6.1: 25–27 (British Council: Madras)

EGAN, R 1986 *The Skilled Helper* (3rd ed.) Wadsworth Inc, Belmont, California

EVERARD, K B and MORRIS, G 1985 *Effective School Management* Harper Education Series

FREEMAN, D 1982 'Observing teachers: three approaches to in-service training and development' *TESOL Quarterly* 16.1: 21–28

FREEMAN, D 1989 'Teacher training, development, and decision making: a model of teaching and related strategies for language teacher education' *TESOL Quarterly* 23.1: 27–45

FREIRE, P 1972 *Pedagogy of the Oppressed* Penguin

GEERTZ, C 1983 *Local Knowledge* Basic Books, New York (esp. Chapter 7, 'The way we think now: toward an ethnography of modern thought')

GENESEE, F 1988 'Neuropsychology and Second Language Acquisition' in BEEBE, L M (ed.) 1988 *Issues in Second Language Acquisition* Newbury House, Rowley, MA

GUBA, E G and LINCOLN, Y S 1982 'Epistemological and methodological bases of naturalistic inquiry' *Educational Communication and Technology Journal* 30.4: 233–252

GUIORA, A Z (ed.) 1983 'An Epistemology for the Language Sciences' *Language Learning* 33.5 (Special Issue)

HANDAL, G and LAUVAS, P 1987 *Promoting Reflective Teaching* Open University Press

HERON, J 1986 *Six Category Intervention Analysis* University of Surrey Human Potential Research Project

HOPKINS, D 1985 *A Teacher's Guide to Classroom Research* Open University Press

KHANUM, T, MALIK, A and SYED, S 1990 'Cooperative Development', *unpublished paper* National Academy for Higher Education, Islamabad

KNAPP, M 1978 (2nd ed.) *Non-Verbal Communication in Human Interaction* Holt Rinehart and Winston, New York

LACEY, C 1990 'Teacher Development: an investigation into Cooperative Development', *unpublished MA dissertation* Birmingham University

VAN LIER, L 1988 *The Classroom and the Language Learner* Longman

LAKOFF, G and JOHNSON, M 1980 *Metaphors We Live By* University of Chicago Press, Chicago

MASLOW, A H 1943 'A theory of human motivation' *Psychological Review* 50: 370–396

MORGAN, J and RINVOLUCRI, M 1986 *Vocabulary* Oxford University Press

MOYLES, J P 1988 *Self-Evaluation: A Primary Teacher's Guide* NFER: Nelson

NELSON-JONES, R 1983 *Practical Counselling Skills* Cassell

NUNAN, D 1989a *Understanding Language Classrooms* Prentice-Hall

NUNAN, D 1989b 'A client-centred approach to teacher development' *ELT Journal* 43.2: 111–119

PEASE, A 1981 *Body Language* Sheldon Press

PLANT, R 1987 *Managing Change and Making it Stick* Fontana

OCHSNER, R 1979 'A poetics of second language acquisition' *Language Learning* 29.1: 53–80

PROGOFF, I 1975 *At a Journal Workshop* Dialogue House, New York

REASON, P (ed.) 1988 *Human Inquiry in Action* Sage

REASON, P and ROWAN, J (eds.) 1981 *Human Inquiry: A Sourcebook of New Paradigm Research* Wiley

RINVOLUCRI, M 1981 'Awareness activities for teaching structures' in EARLY, P (ed.) 1981 *Humanistic Approaches: An Empirical View* ELT Documents 113 (British Council: London)

ROGERS, C 1983 *Freedom to Learn for the Eighties* Merrill, Columbus, Ohio

RUDDOCK, J and HOPKINS, D 1985 *Research as a basis for teaching* Heinemann Educational

SCHÖN, D A 1983 *The Reflective Practitioner: How Professionals Think in Action* Temple Smith

SCOVEL, T 1982 'Questions concerning the application of neurolinguistic research to second language learning/teaching' *TESOL Quarterly* 16.3: 323–331

STEVICK, E W 1980 *Teaching Languages: A Way and Ways* Newbury House, Rowley MA

STEVICK, E W 1990 *Humanism in Language Teaching* Oxford University Press

STONES, E 1984 *Supervision in Teacher Education* Methuen

Teacher Development: The newsletter of the Teacher Development Special Interest Group of the International Association of Teachers of English as a Foreign Language

UNDERHILL, A 1989 'Process in humanistic education' *ELT Journal* 43.4: 250–260

WALLACE, M 1991 *Training for Language Teachers: A Reflective Approach* Oxford University Press

WEEKS, W H, PEDERSEN, P B and BRISLIN, R W (undated) *A Manual of Structured Experiences for Cross-Cultural Learning* Intercultural Press Inc, Yarmouth, Maine

WILLIAMS, M 1989 'A developmental view of classroom observation' *ELT Journal* 43.2: 85–91

WRIGHT, A 1987 *Roles of Teachers and Learners* Oxford University Press

ZDENEK, M 1985 *The Right-Brain Experience* Corgi